# Instant Recovery with Write-Ahead Logging

*Page Repair, System Restart, Media Restore, and System Failover*

Second Edition

# Synthesis Lectures on Data Management

Editor
**Z. Meral Özsoyoğlu**, *Case Western Reserve University*

Founding Editor
**M. Tamer Özsuu**, *University of Waterloo*

**Synthesis Lectures on Data Management** is edited by Meral Özsoyoğlu of Case Western Reserve University. The series publishes 80- to 150-page publications on topics pertaining to data management. Topics include query languages, database system architectures, transaction management, data warehousing, XML and databases, data stream systems, wide scale data distribution, multimedia data management, data mining, and related subjects.

Instant Recovery with Write-Ahead Logging: Page Repair, System Restart, Media Restore, and System Failover
Second Edition
Goetz Graefe, Wey Guy, and Caetano Sauer
March 2016

Veracity of Data: From Truth Discovery Computation Algorithms to Models of Misinformation Dynamics
Laure Berti-Équille, Javier Borge-Holthoefer
December 2015

Datalog and Logic Databases
Sergio Greco, Cristian Molinaro
November 2015

Big Data Integration
Xin Luna Dong, Divesh Srivastava
February 2015

Instant Recovery with Write-Ahead Logging: Page Repair, System Restart, and Media Restore
Goetz Graefe, Wey Guy, and Caetano Sauer
December 2014

Instant Recovery with Write-Ahead Logging: Page Repair, System Restart, Media Restore, and System Failover: Second Edition
Goetz Graefe, Wey Guy, Caetano Sauer


ISBN: 978-3-031-00729-3 print
ISBN: 978-3-031-01857-2 ebook

DOI 10.1007/978-3-031-01857-2

A Publication in the Springer series
*SYNTHESIS LECTURES ON DATA MANAGEMENT #44* Series
Editor: Z. Meral Özsoyoğlu, Case Western Reserve University
Founding Editor: M. Tamer Özsu, University of Waterloo


Series ISSN    2153-5418  Print    2153-5426  Electronic

# Instant Recovery with Write-Ahead Logging

*Page Repair, System Restart, Media Restore, and System Failover*

**Second Edition**

**Goetz Graefe**
Hewlett Packard Labs

**Wey Guy**

**Caetano Sauer**
University of Kaiserslautern

*SYNTHESIS LECTURES ON DATA MANAGEMENT #44*

## ABSTRACT

Traditional theory and practice of write-ahead logging and of database recovery focus on three failure classes: transaction failures (typically due to deadlocks) resolved by transaction rollback; system failures (typically power or software faults) resolved by restart with log analysis, "redo," and "undo" phases; and media failures (typically hardware faults) resolved by restore operations that combine multiple types of backups and log replay.

The recent addition of single-page failures and single-page recovery has opened new opportunities far beyond the original aim of immediate, lossless repair of single-page wear-out in novel or traditional storage hardware. In the contexts of system and media failures, efficient single-page recovery enables on-demand incremental "redo" and "undo" as part of system restart or media restore operations. This can give the illusion of practically instantaneous restart and restore: instant restart permits processing new queries and updates seconds after system reboot and instant restore permits resuming queries and updates on empty replacement media as if those were already fully recovered. In the context of node and network failures, instant restart and instant restore combine to enable practically instant failover from a failing database node to one holding merely an out-of-date backup and a log archive, yet without loss of data, updates, or transactional integrity.

In addition to these instant recovery techniques, the discussion introduces self-repairing indexes and much faster offline restore operations, which impose no slowdown in backup operations and hardly any slowdown in log archiving operations. The new restore techniques also render differential and incremental backups obsolete, complete backup commands on a database server practically instantly, and even permit taking full up-to-date backups without imposing any load on the database server.

Compared to the first version of this book, this second edition adds sections on applications of single-page repair, instant restart, single-pass restore, and instant restore. Moreover, it adds sections on instant failover among nodes in a cluster, applications of instant failover, recovery for file systems and data files, and the performance of instant restart and instant restore.

## KEYWORDS

algorithms, databases, transactions, failures, recovery, availability, reliability, write-ahead logging, instant restart, log analysis, redo, undo, rollback, compensation, log replay, instant restore, single-pass restore, virtual backup, big data, file systems, key-value stores, clusters, log shipping, failover, elasticity, failover pool

# Contents

# Preface

It has been a pleasure developing and compiling this set of concepts and techniques in order to make them available to researchers and software developers around the world. While the foundation of the presented techniques is write-ahead logging as commonly found in database management systems, the techniques and their advantages apply similarly to key-value stores, file systems with journaling, etc.—in other words, to all storage management layers for important and big data. In all these systems, write-ahead logging can enable efficient single-page repair after a localized data loss, system restart after a software crash, and media restore after a failure in the storage hardware or firmware. Instead of copying each data page to multiple devices, as many file storage systems do today in order to achieve high availability, only a single copy is required, plus a log of changes.

# Acknowledgments

Barb Peters and Arianna Lund encouraged combining all "instant recovery" techniques into a single book. Harumi Kuno participated in the research on single-page recovery and its applications.

# CHAPTER 1

# Introduction

Modern hardware differs from hardware of 25 years ago, when many of the database recovery techniques used today were designed. Current hardware includes high-capacity, high-density disks with single-page failures due to cross-track effects, e.g., in shingled or overlapping recording, semiconductor storage with single-page failures due to localized wear-out, large memory and large buffer pools with many pages and therefore many dirty pages and long restart recovery after system failures, and high-capacity storage devices and therefore long restore recovery after media failures.

For example,[1] some of today's servers have 1 TB ($2^{40}$ B) of volatile memory, equal to over 100 million ($2^{27}$) pages of 8 KB ($2^{13}$ B). If 3% (~$2^{-5}$) of these pages are dirty at the time of a system crash, "redo" recovery must inspect and recover several million ($2^{22}$) pages. Even if 16 ($2^4$) devices can each serve 250 ($2^8$) I/O operations per second, the "redo" phase alone of restart recovery takes about 15 minutes ($2^{10}$ seconds). Fewer or slower devices or skew in the access pattern increase "redo" and "undo" times. In contrast, instant restart enables new transactions concurrently to "redo" and "undo" recovery, i.e., several minutes earlier. For a real-world example of the need for fast restart with large memory, some companies see themselves forced to invent special techniques even for clean shutdown and restart, specifically for software upgrade [GCG 14].

As another example, some of today's storage devices hold 4 TB ($2^{42}$ B) of data and transfer data at 250 MB/s ($2^{28}$ B/s). Taking or restoring a full backup takes about 4½ hours ($2^{14}$ seconds). Traditional media recovery starts with a full restore and then requires replaying the recovery log gathered since the last backup, often for many hours. In contrast, instant restore enables transaction processing during the entire restore operation, even permitting active transactions to resume after a very short delay (about a second) rather than abort and eventually restart hours later.

Data and indexes in non-volatile memory do not solve this issue. On one hand, failures and data loss are still possible, albeit with different specific failure modes due to different hardware characteristics. On the other hand, if database backups and log archives reside on traditional disk storage, e.g., in RAID-6 configurations, restore operations and log replay remain limited in bandwidth and take just as long as disk-to-disk recovery. Given the difference in cost per byte for traditional disks and for non-volatile memory, it will be a long time before database backups and log archives will routinely be stored in non-volatile memory.

---

[1] This example, as well as the following one, relies on simple calculations and assumed system parameters. Their purpose is to illustrate orders of magnitude rather than precise values. Readers are welcome to repeat the calculations with alternative parameters or formulas more realistic and more accurate for their computer systems.

This book covers techniques that seem more appropriate for contemporary hardware. It employs and builds on many proven techniques, in particular write-ahead logging, checkpoints, and log archiving. The foundations are two new ideas. First, single-page failures and single-page recovery [GK 12] enable incremental recovery fast enough to run on demand without imposing major delays in query and transaction processing. Second, log archiving not only compresses the log records but also partially sorts the log archive, which enables multiple access patterns, all reasonably efficient. In other words, the contributions of "instant recovery" are ubiquitous fine-grained on-demand recovery and a novel data organization of log archives that permits both efficient archiving, i.e., creation of the log archive, and efficient restore operations, i.e., usage of the log archive.[2]

These foundations are exploited for incremental recovery actions executing on demand, in particular after system failures (producing an impression of "instant restart") and after media failures ("instant restore"). In addition to incremental recovery, new techniques speed up offline backup and offline restore operations. In particular, differential and incremental backups become obsolete and full backups can be created efficiently without imposing any load on the active server process.

Like practically all work on write-ahead logging and recovery using database logs, the new designs assume that the recovery log and the log archive are "stable storage," i.e., free of defects and safe from data loss. With the recovery log and the log archive much smaller than databases and database backups, it seems reasonable to employ highly reliable, available, and redundant hardware as stable storage. The new techniques can recover reliably and efficiently from data loss in databases and backups (assuming older backups are still available) but not from data loss in the recovery log and the log archive.

The problem of out-of-date recovery methods for today's hardware exists equally for file systems, databases, key-value stores, and contents indexes in information retrieval and internet search. Similarly, the techniques and solutions discussed below apply not only to databases, even if they are often discussed using database terms, but also to file systems, key-value stores, and contents indexes. In other words, the problems, techniques, and solutions apply to practically all persistent digital storage technologies that employ write-ahead logging.

Chapter 2 sketches the assumed system context and then reviews related prior work and its influence on instant recovery. Chapter 3 reviews the first step toward seemingly instantaneous recovery, i.e., single-page failures and single-page recovery, and then Chapter 4 introduces applications of single-page recovery after possibly deliberate introduction of single-page failures in the form of out-of-date page on persistent storage. Chapter 5 focuses on instant recovery after a system failure, i.e., restart after a software crash. Chapter 6 suggests applications of instant restart.

---

[2] We use the term "instant" not in an absolute meaning but a relative one, i.e., in comparison to prior techniques. This is like instant coffee, which is not absolutely instantaneous but only relative to traditional techniques of coffee preparation. The reader's taste and opinion must decide whether instant coffee actually is coffee. Instant recovery, however, is true and reliable recovery from system and media failures, with guarantees as strong as those of traditional recovery techniques.

Chapter 7 introduces new techniques for offline restore operations and Chapter 8 introduces applications of the new restore techniques, including "instant backup" techniques that prepare a full and current backup in seconds rather than hours. Chapter 9 introduces "instant restore" techniques for high-availability recovery from media failures and Chapter 10 describes specific applications of instant restore. Chapter 11 considers multiple failure including media failures during system restart and system failures during media restore operations. Chapter 12 combines single-page repair, instant restart, single-pass restore, and instant restore into a design for instant failover; with Chapter 13 covering some applications of instant failover. Chapter 14 extends the recovery techniques from databases to file systems including data pages that lack page headers and thus PageLSN values. Chapter 15 gives some illustrative performance examples, in particular for instant restart, single-pass restore, and instant restore. Chapter 16 offers a summary of the book.

CHAPTER  2

# Related Prior Work

Instant recovery and related techniques employ a wide variety of established techniques for transactions, concurrency control, logging, and recovery [HR 83]. The following discussion covers the principal ones among them: the set of techniques known as ARIES; traditional techniques for restart, backup, and restore operations; database maintenance with allocation-only logging; and system transactions as a special form of open nested transactions.

## 2.1    SYSTEM MODEL

The following discussions assume a simple database system or key-value store implemented on a conventional computer system. The principal hardware assumptions include page-access persistent storage and a buffer pool in volatile memory. Moreover, there is no hardware or software replication or mirroring, except that storage of log records is very reliable. The required "stable storage" is often realized by mirrored storage just for the recovery log and, if one exists, the log archive. The techniques in this book do not address failures in the recovery log or in the log archive, instead assuming the fiction of "stable storage" just like prior research and commercial work on database recovery. Similarly, the techniques in this book do not address memory failures, i.e., correctness of volatile memory such as traditional DRAM.

The only form of redundant storage is write-ahead logging supporting transactions, commit log records, in-place updates of pages and records, "exactly once" log records including compensation log records, and checkpoints. Transactions support all ACID properties: atomicity ("all or nothing"), consistency, isolation (concurrency control), and durability (persistence). The software must guarantee failure atomicity is guaranteed even in cases of transaction failures (rollback), system failures (e.g., operating system crash), media failures (e.g., head scratch), and single-page failures (e.g., local wear). Concurrency control may employ page-level locking but also record-level locking, key-value locking, and key-range locking.

Figure 2.1 illustrates the principal data structures participating in update processing, system restart after system failures, and restore operations after media failures. Transaction logic modifies images of database pages in the buffer pool and writes appropriate log records to the recovery log. Database backups provide long-term storage for database contents and the log archive provides long-term storage for log records. In case of a system failure, system restart ensures up-to-date buffer pool contents from the available database and the recovery log, along with other server state in the transaction manager and the lock manager. In case of a media failure, restore operations combine database backups and log archive into an up-to-date replacement database. Verbs associated with the arrows are (counter-clockwise from the top) to log updates and to apply log records, to read and write database pages, to back up the database, to restore a database backup, to replay the log, and to archive the log.

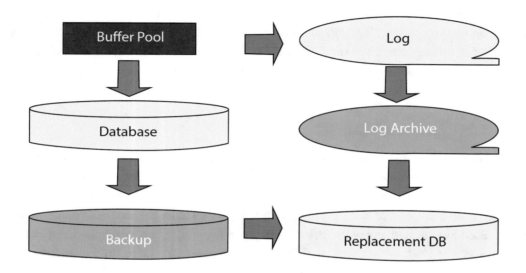

Figure 2.1: System model and update progagation.

Any or all of the data structures in Figure 2.1 could reside in non-volatile memory. For the time being, the difference in latency between traditional and non-volatile memory suggests a buffer pool in traditional memory even for persistent data in non-volatile memory. For buffer pool management, as well as for fault containment and efficient repair, page-like containers will move between traditional memory and non-volatile memory. The difference in cost (per capacity) between traditional disk and non-volatile memory suggests database backups and log archive on traditional disks or disk arrays. The recovery log is the best and the database is the next-best candidate for non-volatile memory. In order to use non-volatile memory as effectively as possible, log records in non-volatile memory will migrate quickly to the log archive and only "warm" database pages will reside in non-volatile memory, with hot pages in traditional memory and cold pages on flash or disk media. Note that references among pages both in traditional and non-volatile memory may employ virtual memory pointers rather than traditional database addresses such as page identifiers on disk. With respect to the recovery topics covered here, non-volatile memory will not invalidate the system model of Figure 2.1 and the new techniques readily apply to systems with non-volatile memory, e.g., instant restart and instant restore using write-ahead logging rather than redundant mirrors. For the foreseeable future, multiple copies (mirrors) of entire databases in non-volatile memory will be cost effective only for extremely specialized applications.

In a distributed system or a cluster, the techniques below apply to each node or instance. Database replication, e.g., to multiple nodes in a cluster, is no longer required if recovery from system and media failures is nearly instantaneous and if database backups and log archives are reliable, e.g., by redundancy in disk arrays. Instant failover, i.e., new cross-node recovery techniques, eschews continuous updates to multiple database copies and instead relies on techniques from instant restart and instant restore based on continuous log shipping (Chapter 12).

## 2.2    ARIES

ARIES [MHL 92] is commonly used for logging and recovery in databases and other data management software. It relies on write-ahead logging [G 78]. In prior designs, a failed transaction rolls back by reverting database pages to their prior state. This approach does not work correctly if two transactions update the same page concurrently; thus, prior designs force page-level locking. In contrast, ARIES enables fine granularities of locking, e.g., row-level locking (ARIES/IM [ML 92]) and key-value locking (ARIES/KVL [M 90]). Transaction rollback is logical, i.e., it performs the reversing update and writes a compensation log record.

Each log record describing a transaction update points to the most recent prior log record of the same transaction. Each compensation log record includes a field called "next undo lsn" (a log sequence number is the address of a log record within the recovery log), which guides rollback after an interruption, e.g., a system failure during transaction rollback. Each database page contains a PageLSN field that indicates the most recent log record reflected in the page image, enabling "exactly once" application of log records to database pages.

```
Begin transaction
Update page 7, slot 9: ...
Update page 4, slot 6: ...
Rollback
Rollback
Commit (nothing)
```

Figure 2.2: Write-ahead logging and compensation log records.

Figure 2.2 shows log records for a transaction that first updates two records in a database, then decides to abort, therefore logs two rollback actions, and finally commits. The initial log records contain both "redo" and "undo" information, i.e., both new values and old values. The decision to abort the transaction does not require a log record; due to "all or nothing" failure atomicity, any transaction and its updates are invalid until the recovery log contains a commit log record for the transaction. The rollback log records, called "compensation log records" in ARIES, can refer to the original log records for some or all of the required "undo" information. In some cases, the rollback is logical. For example, if the original update modified a b-tree entry and then another transaction moves this entry to another page as part of a node split, rolling back the original update requires updating a page other than the original one. Thus, ARIES compensation log records always contain all information required to repeat a rollback action and do not point to the original log record. Instead, they point to the preceding log record with their "next undo lsn" field. The final log record in Figure 2.2 completes the transaction abort. The example recovery log shows it as a commit log record because the transaction leaves no updates in the database after rolling back each of its updates; in that sense, there is no difference between commit and abort. Differently from a successful transaction, the database can acknowledge transaction abort to the user or application immediately without waiting for this commit log record to reach stable storage.

ARIES "top-level actions" are quite similar to "open nested transactions" [M 06]. They run on behalf of a user transaction and in the same thread yet their results are visible to other threads and transactions and they do not roll back when the user transaction rolls back. They are extremely useful for contents-neutral database maintenance, e.g., splitting a b-tree node, and in many ways similar to system transactions described in Section 2.8.

Numerous articles augment and optimize the original ARIES design. For example, the "commit lsn" technique [M 90b] permits omission of (read-only) locking and even latching for database pages unmodified for longer than the age of the oldest active transaction—if a database page has not been modified concurrently to any active transaction, then no active transaction can hold an exclusive lock on the page. Another optimization for "fast availability during restart" [M 93] permits new transactions very quickly after a system failure and restart—based on the "commit lsn" technique, it gives access to all database pages except those updated recently, which may well be the application's working set.

A notable extension of ARIES by others than the original authors is "C-ARIES" (concurrent ARIES recovery) [SK 07]. In that design, both "redo" and "undo" partition their work by database page, with a thread per page and all pages in recovery at the same time. Individual pages become available to new transactions as threads complete their work. Concerns with this design include massive resource usage (many threads), completion in random order (as threads finish; not as needed by new user transactions), and restriction to page-level locking without support for record-level locking or key-value locking in b-tree indexes.

## 2.3    RESTART AFTER A SYSTEM FAILURE

Traditional recovery from a system failure (e.g., a crash of the operating system) proceeds in three phases: log analysis, physical "redo," and logical "undo" by compensation. Log analysis and "redo" may use the same log scan, but there are good reasons for separate scans and phases. Log analysis without immediate "redo" is very quick as it merely reads the log sequentially, whereas "redo" performance is limited by many random reads in the database.

```
T₁: Begin transaction
T₁: Update page 7, slot 9: ...
Database checkpoint
T₁: Update page 4, slot 6: ...
T₂: Begin transaction
T₂: Update page 3, slot 1: ...
Written page 7
T₁: Rollback
T₂: Update page 4, slot 6: ...
T₁: Rollback
T₁: Commit (nothing)
```

Figure 2.3: Example recovery log.

Figure 2.3 shows an example recovery log, extended from the example in Figure 2.2. In addition to log records describing updates of database pages and records (each with a transaction identifier $T_1$ or $T_2$), this recovery log contains a database checkpoint, a write confirmation, and a transaction end after successful transaction rollback. Updates and rollback actions are associated with specific transactions; checkpoints and write actions describe server activity and thus have no associated transactions.

Log analysis scans all log records from the most recent checkpoint to the system failure. Information in the checkpoint initializes some server state, in particular in the transaction manager, the lock manager, and the buffer pool. In its scan, log analysis finds additional active transactions, identifies committed transactions ("winner" transactions), and ends with a list of incomplete transactions ("loser" transactions). In addition, it builds a list of pages possibly in need of "redo" recovery ("in-doubt" pages). Some database systems log completed writes to the database, which permits the log analysis logic to remove entries from this list of in-doubt database pages. Figure 2.3 shows an example log record for database page 7.

The "redo" phase ensures that database pages reflect all log records prior to the system failure (physical "redo"). The "undo" phase then rolls back all incomplete transactions, including those that started prior to the most recent checkpoint. Rollback compensates or "updates back" what these transactions modified in the database. For example, a node split in a b-tree may have moved a record from one page to another between initial update (during forward processing or "redo" recovery) and compensating update (logical "undo"). Of course, these cases can only occur with a fine granularity of locking, i.e., record-level locking (or key-value locking in indexes, or key-range in b-tree indexes) rather than page-, index-, or table-level locking.

After all recovery phases are complete, most systems take a checkpoint and then admit new transactions. With lock acquisition in the "redo" phase, new transactions may overlap the "undo" phase [MHL 92]. A refinement of this work [M 93] permits new transactions earlier, i.e., even during the "redo" phase, but only if they do not touch database pages that might require "redo" recovery, which is determined using the PageLSN of the database page and a global variable "commit lsn." If a new transaction attempts to access a page possibly in need of "redo" recovery, the transaction must abort or wait until recovery is complete. In contrast, the techniques of Chapter 5 permit new transactions to query and update any database page, including those affected by "redo" and "undo" recovery.

Figure 2.4: Traditional restart phases.

Figure 2.4 illustrates the three phases of traditional restart after a crash, i.e., recovery from a system failure, and some typical durations. The first phase reads the recovery log written before the crash, starting with the most recent completed checkpoint and ending with the last log record. This phase is very short because it does not read database pages and it does not write new log records. Moreover, the frequency of checkpoints during transaction processing controls the duration of log analysis after a crash. The first phase may end with taking a new checkpoint. The second phase scans the pre-crash recovery log again, reads database pages into the buffer pool, and ensures that page images in the database or at least in the buffer pool reflect all pre-crash updates. This phase takes much longer due to random I/O in the database, although frequent checkpoints can limit its duration. The third phase scans the pre-crash recovery log backward, starting with the last log record, and rolls back loser transactions. The duration or size (count of log records) of the loser transactions controls the duration of the "undo" phase. The frequency of checkpoints has no effect. New checkpoints are possible throughout the "redo" and "undo" phases.

Shore [CDF 94, JPH 09] uses unique logic during the "undo" phase, which avoids the need for backward scan logic. It rolls back all actions of loser transactions in the reverse order of original execution. It does not roll back one transaction at a time. Instead, Shore rolls back transactions in an interleaved schedule, precisely reversing their pre-crash history. The control logic of rollback traverses the per-transaction linked lists of log records for all failed transactions and merges them, using a priority queue quite similar to the merge logic in an external merge sort.

Shore code comments mention this specific concern against rolling back one transaction at a time during system restart: rollback of a deletion may fail if an insertion has taken up the space and the database may have no further free space available for the re-insertion reversing the deletion. There might have been alternative solutions for this specific issue, e.g., use of ghost records with system transactions reclaiming the space only after user transactions end. Transactions growing and shrinking records can create a very similar problem. A possible solution is "ghost space" within database records such that user transactions only modify allocated space, delegating all allocation operations to system transactions, which never require rollback if a single log record describes the entire system transaction including its commit. Moreover, if this concern is real for transaction-by-transaction rollback during restart, it seems that a particularly unfortunate sequence of transaction aborts might create the same problem even without system failure and restart. In other words, solving this problem only for restart is not sufficient.

The root cause of these concerns is rollback of multiple failed transactions in an unpredictable order different from the reverse of their original schedule. A possible remedy is to delegate all space management to system transactions, permitting user transactions only to modify allocated space. This must range from a few bytes within a record (perhaps named "ghost space") to records within a page (known as ghost records or "pseudo-deleted" records) and to entire indexes in a database: index removal only marks the index a ghost such that one or more system transactions can return all the index pages to free space management. If so, user transactions can roll back in any order without concerns for space management, for allocation errors, etc. This includes parallel restart recovery using multiple threads, typically with parallel "redo" by partitioning database pages and parallel "undo" by partitioning transactions.

## 2.4    DATABASE BACKUP AND LOG ARCHIVE

Traditional strategies against data loss have focused on prevention rather than repair of media failures. For example, redundancy in the form of disk mirroring (originally known as shadowing [BG 88] and later as RAID-1 [CLG 94]) or parity (RAID-4/5/6) attempts to prevent media failure visible to a database system by providing recovery at a lower system level, i.e., storage software or file system. Nonetheless, computer failures do happen, and database backups are standard operating procedure. Note that recovery techniques below the database often cannot ensure that the effects of all committed database transactions are preserved; thus, recovery in the database level is often required for transactional correctness.

Three forms of backups are commonly used: a full backup saves all allocated database pages, a differential backup saves all database pages modified since the last full backup, and an incremental backup saves only those database pages modified since the last backup of any kind. Thus, the size of a full backup principally equals that of the database, the size of a differential backup grows due to additional transactional updates, and the size of regular incremental backups is proportional to the update workload.

Backup operations usually compress their output. This starts with skipping over database pages not allocated to any table or index and suppressing free space within database pages. For example, after many random updates, b-tree nodes remain only ~70% full. Thereafter, all standard compression techniques apply. Compression of backups is not possible in incrementally updated backups, a feature in a product that overwrites pages in a full backup with page images from an incremental backup.

Backup operations may be offline or online, i.e., permitting concurrent database updates including start and commit of transactions. Online backup operations also log their start and end. These log records control compression and aggregation in the log archiving process.

An offline backup captures all database pages at a particular point in time, defined by a single LSN value. All updates logged prior to that log record are included in the backup, whereas subsequent updates are not. A restore operation targeting such a backup point requires rollback of incomplete transactions. The required information is quite similar to that logged in a traditional checkpoint. While an offline backup operation permits incomplete transactions but no new log records during the backup operation, an online backup permits new updates and thus extends this point to an interval. All log records written during an online backup operation must be preserved in order to enable correct log replay during recovery from any page version that the backup may include. A restore operation must attempt to apply the log records written during the backup operation.

The three types of database backups also differ in the data structures they require within a database. A full backup requires only the data structures also needed for free space management. Differential and incremental backups, however, require additional bitmaps (one bit per database page). Only a full backup resets the bitmap for differential backups but any backup resets the bitmap for incremental backups. Online incremental backups require two bitmaps, one guiding the active backup and one gathering page identifiers for the next incremental backup. When an online incremental backup fails, these bitmaps must be merged. Efficient non-redundant maintenance of these bitmaps during transaction processing exploits PageLSN values [MN 93]. Only the first update after a backup operation needs to modify the bitmap; subsequent updates can compare the PageLSN value with the LSN values of the relevant backup operations. Note also that these bitmaps and all logic for maintenance and reset would be obsolete if differential and incremental backups could become obsolete

While backups provide long-term storage of the database, the log archive provides long-term storage of the recovery log. Latency-optimized devices typically hold the recovery log, e.g., flash or soon non-volatile memory, whereas devices optimized for reliability and cost, e.g., RAID-6 arrays, hold the log archive. Continuous log archiving permits recycling space on the latency-optimized logging devices.

Traditional log archiving merely copies the recovery log. Standard compression techniques may reduce bandwidth and space requirements. In addition, log archiving may suppress all information irrelevant for media recovery, e.g., log records for transaction start and end, transaction identifiers within log records, "undo" information of committed transactions, server state information such as checkpoint log records, etc. Gray [G 78] suggests sorting all log records and suppressing all but the latest log record for each page, assuming full-page logging (entire database pages in each log record) and thus page-level locking (not record-level locking or key-value locking).

## 2.5   RESTORE AFTER A MEDIA FAILURE

After a media failure that lower system levels cannot mask, e.g., RAID arrays, database recovery based on backups, log archive, and recovery log takes over. Assuming replacement media that are ready, i.e., formatted but empty, restore operations proceed through a full backup, a differential backup if available, and incremental backups, followed by replaying the log since the last backup. The final step is to roll back incomplete transactions.

The "redo" phase of restore operations may need to repeat many hours of archived log records. Due to the required random I/O operations in the database, log replay may take nearly as many hours as the original transaction execution. For example, with daily backups, log replay may take close to a day.

The "undo" phase of restore operations may need to wait until log replay is complete. Thus, database transactions with locks and pending updates on the failed device may remain suspended for many hours.

Figure 2.5: Traditional restore phases.

Figure 2.5 illustrates typical phases of restore operations. Not all phases are present in all cases; for example, database administrators use either differential or incremental backups, but not both. Section 8.4 suggests an alternative to both differential and incremental backups. The initial restore operation from the most recent full backup can take multiple hours, depending on the capacity and sustained bandwidth of the failed device. For example, writing with a sustained bandwidth of 100 MB/s for an hour restores 360 GB; a 4 TB device at 250 MB/s requires about 4½ hours. The "redo" phase, also known as log replay, also can take hours, primarily due to many random I/O operations. In extreme situations, it can take nearly as much time as transaction processing that wrote the log. In some cases, it may save time to select log records pertaining to the failed device, sort them by page identifier, and then apply them in a single sweep over the address space. Gray [G 78] wrote: "For disk objects, log records can be sorted by cylinder, then track, then sector, then time. … Since it is sorted by physical address, media recovery becomes a merge of the image dump of the object and its change accumulation tape." Gray did not consider differential or incremental backups; if those are sorted by page identifier, all backups can be merged for a single restore operation. The transactions active at the time of the device failure must wait for the replacement device and the restore operation; once the "redo" phase is complete, clean rollback of these transactions becomes possible.

Some database products sort log records in order to speed up log replay after restoring backups.[3] They follow and implement Gray's ideas above, augmenting them with asynchronous bulk read-ahead, but do not fully exploit the opportunities and techniques essential for single-pass restore, e.g., splitting an external merge sort into run generation during log archiving and merging during restore (Chapter 7), or for instant restore, e.g., indexing backups and log archive (Chapter 9).

Other database products support features somewhat comparable to single-page recovery (Chapter 3), but with much simpler and slower functionality. For example, the "restore" command of Microsoft SQL Server [M 12] permits a set of page identifiers as a selection predicate applied to log records during a scan of log backups and the recovery log. In other words, single-page recovery is neither automatic (an explicit command is required) nor efficient (entire logs are scanned, with log records for all pages on all devices). Microsoft recommends this feature only for small sets of database pages, certainly not as part of recovery from a media failure as in instant restore (Chapter 9).

## 2.6    MIRRORING, LOG SHIPPING, AND FAILOVER

Traditional techniques for high availability require one or more secondary servers running on separate nodes in a cluster or in separate failure domains, even in remote data centers. Each secondary server holds a complete copy of the database and keeps it up-to-date at all times. Maintenance of

---

[3] In IBM DB2 for z/OS, for example, "Prior to V6, the log apply process was I/O bound. As each log record was read, the data page it applied to was retrieved from the DB2 buffer pool or read from [disk] and changed as required ([…]). The next log record was read and the process was repeated, with each data page read synchronously. Also, because many different log records could apply to the same data page, pages could be read many times. Fast log apply uses multitasking (one log-read subtask and one or more log-apply subtasks). List pre-fetch (which can be thought of as an intelligent channel command word in that non-contiguous pages can be read in one read operation) is used to significantly reduce synchronous-read operations. Fast log apply also reduces the number of times pages are read by sorting together groups of log records that apply to the same page or set of pages before applying the changes." [S 05]

such secondary database copies may rely on writing each dirty database page not only to the primary database copy but also to each secondary copy. Alternatively, the primary database server may send its log records to all secondary servers, which apply those log records to their local database copy in continuous log replay and "redo" recovery. Common names for these alternative techniques are database mirroring and log shipping, respectively. Both techniques require an up-to-date database and lots of I/O on each secondary server. Log shipping saves network bandwidth by shipping log records rather than entire database pages but it requires reading database pages in addition to writing them and it requires processing log records and their "redo" actions.

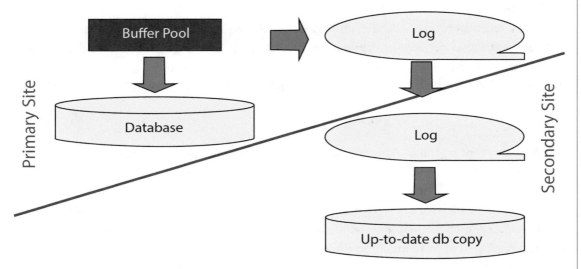

Figure 2.6: Traditional log shipping.

Figure 2.6 illustrates the concept, with a diagonal red line separating the primary and secondary sites. The primary sites processes updates requested by users and applications, generates log records and ships them across the network to all secondary sites. Each secondary site reads the required database pages from its local copy of the database, applies the log record, and writes the modified back to its local database.

When the primary database server or its network connection fails, a secondary server takes over. Typically, the new primary server rolls back all incomplete transactions. Failovers that resume active transactions require not only tight synchronization among servers but also failover of all communication, connections, and logins. There may be special rules and implementation techniques for long-running operations that modify the database representation but not its logical contents, e.g., index creation or database defragmentation.

When a database update transaction commits on the primary server, one of multiple events may let its transaction manager acknowledge the commit to the user or application. The most eager alternative acknowledges the commit immediately when the commit log record is in the local recovery log. An intermediate alternative acknowledges the commit when one or more secondary servers have acknowledged receipt of the commit log record. The most conservative alternative acknowledges the commit only after all secondary servers have written the commit log record to their local copies of the recovery log. These choices affect the commit delay as experienced by users and applications as well as the strength of the transactional durability guarantee in cases of node or network failures.

If a secondary server is under-utilized by merely receiving and applying log records, it can also serve as primary database server for other database partitions or it can serve as read-only query processing server based on its local copy of the database. The latter choice can provide scalability even for databases with complex update workloads that render database partitioning difficult.

## 2.7    ALLOCATION-ONLY LOGGING

Many database management systems support some database modifications without logging records and page contents, instead logging only allocation actions and the database updates that bring newly allocated pages into existing data structures. For example, splitting a b-tree node requires allocation and formatting of a new page, moving records from the overflowing b-tree node to the new node, and integrating the new node within the b-tree structure. Allocation-only logging suppresses detailed logging of record removal in the old node and record insertion in the new node. Instead, the log record indicates only the page identifiers and the record count or the new boundary key value. Allocation, formatting, and pointer adjustments within the b-tree write log records as usual, albeit perhaps with some special compression.

Operations with allocation-only logging are also known as "non-logged operations" or "minimally logged operations." In addition to page operations like load balancing among b-tree nodes, it applies to creation and removal of redundant data structures (e.g., "non-logged index creation"), to loading new data, and to purging out-of-date data, e.g., in a data warehouse that covers at all times only the most recent 24 months.

Load operations may employ allocation-only logging only for newly allocated pages. Updates of pre-existing pages require traditional log records. For example, allocation-only logging applies to a new leaf node in a b-tree but insertion of a pointer to the new leaf node in a pre-existing branch node requires a traditional log record. For load operations into non-empty tables, traditional indexes do not support allocation-only logging. In contrast, partitioned b-trees [G 03] permit allocation-only logging while loading new data into a dedicated delta partition.

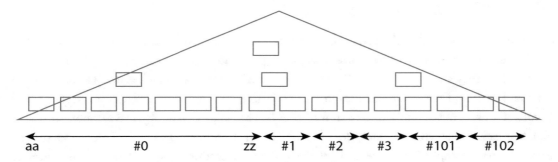

Figure 2.7: Partitioned b-tree after loading into dedicated delta partitions.

Figure 2.7 shows a partitioned b-tree as a triangle with individual (root, branch, and leaf) pages suggested by boxes and the overall b-tree suggested by a triangle. A partitioned b-tree is an ordinary b-tree except for an artificial leading key field in each record, which serves as partition identifier. All records with the same partition identifier are contiguous within the b-tree order. Partition boundaries may or may not coincide with leaf page boundaries. Within each partition, records are sorted according to the user-defined index key, suggested in Figure 2.7 by key values aa and zz for partition #0 only. One of the partitions within the b-tree, which is marked #0 in the diagram and in the artificial leading key field of all its records, contains all the long-existing data records. A single large load operation has recently loaded two delta partitions, marked #101 to #102. Their individual sizes reflect the workspace used for sorting (run generation) within the load operation. Other delta partitions, marked #1 to #3, hold recent insertions by various small transactions. Among all these partitions, #0 is used in read-only mode until a general merge and reorganization operation occurs. As multiple transactions have modified the pages of partitions #1 to #3, these transactions employed standard locking and logging. The dedicated delta partitions #101 to #102 may be locked as units, e.g., by key-value locking on distinct values in the artificial leading key field, and may be loaded with allocation-only logging.

For recovery from system failures, committing load operations with allocation-only logging must force new data pages to permanent storage. For recovery from media failures, the log archive must include not only the log records from the recovery log but also the newly allocated data pages. In other words, until a database backup or the log archive have saved the new data pages, a media failure implies data loss. For load operations, this is usually an acceptable risk, in particular if the data source of the load operation remains available.

## 2.8    SYSTEM TRANSACTIONS

[4]System transactions modify the physical representation of a database but they must not affect the logical database contents. In other words, users and applications do not care about system transactions, whether they are committed or aborted, when and how they are invoked, etc. Users care only inasmuch as system transactions enable efficient and successful completion of user transactions. For example, if a user transaction requests an insertion but the appropriate physical location such as a b-tree leaf lacks sufficient free space, then the user transaction may invoke a system transaction to create free space by splitting the leaf. After the system transaction logs its changes and commits, the user transaction can resume and succeed.

When a user transaction invokes a system transaction, it waits for the system transaction to complete. Thus, the system transaction can run within the same software thread and the invocation overhead is negligible. Moreover, if concurrency control for data structures (also known as latching) depends on threads, a system transaction can immediately use latched data structures just like the user transaction. For example, if a user transaction has latched a b-tree leaf page with insufficient free space and invoked a system transaction to remedy the situation, there is no need to acquire the same latch again.

A system transaction must log its database changes, reverse them upon failure, and insert a commit record into the recovery log upon completion. There is no need, however, to force the commit record to stable storage upon commit. This is because system transactions are limited to representation changes, with no change in logical database contents. Thus, users and applications never rely on completion and durability of system transactions for correct query results or logical database contents. Forcing their commit records to stable storage would render small system transactions unacceptably expensive and practically useless; avoiding this expense permits efficient database implementations with liberal use of small system transactions. In fact, there are cases where a system transaction may invoke another system transaction, i.e., system transactions may be nested.

Table 2.1 lists many of the differences between user transactions and system transactions. More detail and discussion can be found elsewhere [G 12].

---

[4]  Most of this section is derived from [G 12].

Table 2.1: User transactions vs. system transactions

|  | User transactions | System transactions |
|---|---|---|
| Invocation source | User requests | System-internal logic |
| Database effects | Logical database contents | Physical data structure |
| Data location | Database or buffer pool | In-memory page images |
| Scope | Unlimited | 1–3 database pages (usually) |
| Duration | Unlimited, until user's commit request | One short critical section |
| Parallelism | Multiple threads possible | Single thread |
| Invocation overhead | New thread | Same thread |
| Locks | Acquire and retain | Test for conflicting locks |
| Commit overhead | Force log to stable storage, or wait in "group commit" | No forcing, no waiting |
| Logging | Full "redo" and "undo" | Omit "undo" in many cases |
| Recovery | Backward | Forward or backward |
| Hardware support | Non-volatile memory | Transactional memory |

Contrasting system transactions, as described above, from "top-level actions" in ARIES yields the following similarities and differences. Both focus on database representation rather than user-visible contents changes. System transactions require their data in memory, including in-memory images of disk pages, whereas "top-level actions" have no such requirement, perhaps because it would not have been acceptable 25 years ago when ARIES was designed. ARIES introduces "instant locks" whereas system transactions verify an appropriate server state, which may include absence of conflicting locks. In other words, system transactions retain latches to the end of a critical section and permit retaining all locks to the end of a transaction. Finally, ARIES top-level actions require dummy log records and "next undo LSN" backward pointers to skip log records correctly when "undo"ing (compensating) a user transaction whereas system transactions, by virtue of being separate transactions, require neither dummy log records nor backward pointers. In summary, system transactions and ARIES top-level actions are similar in intent and scope but quite different in their details, with system transactions deriving most of their properties and implementation requirements from the fact that they are independent transactions.

System transactions should perform all allocation actions, e.g., transfer of page ownership between free space management and a storage structure, creation and removal of ghost records, growing and shrinking records, etc. User transactions should merely modify allocated space and existing structures, e.g., toggling a "ghost bit" in an existing record or using "ghost space" within a record to resize a variable-size field.

## 2.9    SUMMARY OF PRIOR WORK

In summary, robust techniques are in daily use for recovery from system and media failures. It might seem that further improvements are unlikely or of limited value. The following chapters aim to prove this point of view wrong. After a discussion of single-page failures, single-page recovery, and some specific applications, subsequent chapters exploit single-page recovery for on-demand, incremental recovery from system and media failures, thus enabling the appearance of instant recovery with new queries and transactions practically immediately after system reboot or media replacement.

CHAPTER 3

# Single-Page Recovery

[5]Modern hardware such as flash storage promises higher performance than traditional hardware such as rotating magnetic disks. However, it also introduces its own issues such as relatively high write costs and limited endurance. Techniques such as log-structured file systems and write-optimized b-trees [G 04] might reduce the effects of high write costs and wear leveling might delay the onset of reliability problems. Nonetheless, when failures do occur, they must be identified and repaired.

Failure of individual pages on storage such as flash is not properly described by any of the traditional failure classes considered in transaction processing and database systems. Single-page failures are substantially different from transaction failures, from media failures, and from system failures. Among those three traditional failure classes, single-page failures are most similar to media failures. They differ from media failures, however, since only individual pages fail, not an entire device. Treating one or a few failed pages as a failure of the entire device seems very wasteful. In a system that relies on flash memory for all its storage, doing so would turn a single-page failure into a system-wide hardware failure. Similarly, in a traditional parallel server with single-disk nodes, a single-page failure would turn into a node failure. The problem in these cases is that traditional techniques treat single-page failures as media failures.

## 3.1 DETECTION OF SINGLE-PAGE FAILURES

Every database system includes a consistency check for on-storage data structures, including indexes, tables, catalogs, free space management, and more. There are many possible causes for inconsistencies, from hardware defects and firmware defects in networking or storage hardware to software defects in the database management system, in the operating system, in the storage or replication software, etc. [M 95]. While some system layers have their own consistency checks, e.g., disk drives, those can detect problems only within their own scope and domain. Given how much effort is spent on consistency checks in product development, in production servers, in user groups, etc., it is surprising how little research and literature exists on the topic [GS 09].

Another alternative is continuous checking, e.g., upon each I/O operation or even during each root-to-leaf b-tree traversal in an index such as a b-tree. For storage media with endurance concerns and local failures, e.g., flash storage, each read operation (from storage into the buffer pool) should trigger consistency checking. If memory errors (and thus the buffer pool) are a con-

---

[5]  Most of this chapter is derived from [GK 12].

cern, each root-to-leaf traversal should check page consistency, which not only verifies the page contents but also loads it into the CPU cache such that memory errors do not affect the search within the page. Previous work [GKK 12, GS 09] determined that the cost of checking fields in the page header is moderate, but that checking all intra-page invariants including sort order and space management during each root-to-leaf traversal is too expensive in all but extreme situations, e.g., during system development and debugging.

## 3.2    RECOVERY FOR LOGGED UPDATES

Single-page recovery uses a page image in a backup and the history of the page as captured in the recovery log, specifically the "redo" portions of log records pertaining to the specific database page. Efficient access to all relevant log records requires a pointer to the most recent log record and, within each log record, a pointer to the prior one.

The original proposal for single-page failures suggests a "page recovery index" for each database or each table space. With an index entry for each page in the database or table space, an entry in the page recovery index points to the most recent log record for each database not in the buffer pool. In other words, each time the buffer pool writes a dirty database page to storage, an entry in the page recovery index requires an update with a new LSN value.

For the per-page list of log records, each log record merely embeds the PageLSN value found before the log record's update. In other words, this value is easy to obtain during transaction processing and it can serve other purposes than single-page recovery. These include consistency checking during log-based replication and during log replay while restoring a failed storage device. The recovery logs of Oracle and Microsoft databases contain per-page chains of log records, although not for single-page recovery.

Lookup in the page recovery index, in a backup file, and in the log record might require multiple I/O operations. While seemingly expensive at first sight, it is cheap and efficient when compared to data loss or device mirroring with doubled costs from initial hardware acquisition to each write operation.

## 3.3    RECOVERY FOR NON-LOGGED UPDATES

Allocation-only logging applies to contents-neutral page operations and index operations. Prototypical examples include moving a page (as used in defragmentation and reorganization), splitting a b-tree node (including load balancing), adaptive merging in a partitioned b-tree [G 12], and creation of a new secondary index.

In traditional load balancing with allocation-only logging, the source page must remain unchanged until the destination page is safe. In a database with many independent updates, this limitation is difficult to enforce as it might require a write operation for the destination page when an application requires updating the source page.

In an alternative design, e.g., for splitting a node in a b-tree, page operations produce multiple new pages, retaining and freezing a copy of the original page. O'Neil's SB-trees [O 92], which manage extents on disk pages akin to records in b-tree pages, may alleviate the concerns about contiguity on disk and about scan performance. The original page copy becomes obsolete when both new pages are in the database, in a backup, or in the log archive. If single-page recovery becomes necessary, it repeats history starting from the original page copy.

For index operations, the source must similarly remain frozen until the destination, e.g., a new secondary index, is saved in the database or in the log archive. If the index operation requires a sort operation with temporary file, e.g., runs in an external merge sort, those, too, could play a role in specialized recovery logic. However, the complexity of designing, implementing, and testing this logic, together with the need to place run files not in temporary storage but in persistent database storage, renders this approach unpractical. On the other hand, if index creation merely extracts and saves index entries, leaving them for example in runs or partitions in a partitioned b-tree, then index optimization (merging runs or key ranges within runs) can proceed with allocation-only logging, leaving the original runs in place in case they are needed as backup pages in subsequent single-page recovery [GS 13].

## 3.4    CHAINS OF LOG RECORDS

Today's recovery logs include per-transaction chains of log records, i.e., each log record contains the log sequence number of the prior log record of the same transaction. These chains seem required for efficient transaction rollback. They are not required in the permanent recovery log, however, if the transaction manager can, for each active transaction, retain equivalent information in memory, e.g., in the transaction manager. This seems possible because most transactions require less than a dozen log records such that a small data structure in the transaction manager suffices. Large transactions often employ allocation-only logging such that the number of log records per large transaction remains small.

Figure 3.1 illustrates the traditional design with each log record in a persistent recovery log pointing to the preceding log record of the same transaction. The exceptions are compensation log records. In a design with system transactions, they may point to the original log record as shown. In the ARIES design with top-level actions, compensation log records and their "next undo lsn" field point to the log record next requiring rollback.

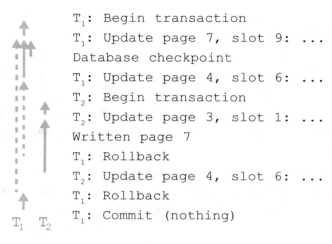

```
T₁: Begin transaction
T₁: Update page 7, slot 9: ...
Database checkpoint
T₁: Update page 4, slot 6: ...
T₂: Begin transaction
T₂: Update page 3, slot 1: ...
Written page 7
T₁: Rollback
T₂: Update page 4, slot 6: ...
T₁: Rollback
T₁: Commit (nothing)
```

Figure 3.1: Per-transaction chain of log records.

Recovery from system failures might use the per-transaction chains of log records, e.g., as described in Section 2.3 for Shore. However, log analysis can re-create the equivalent in-memory data structures in the transaction manager during its log scan, just as it re-creates other in-memory server state from the scanned log records. In order to initialize log analysis, checkpoint log records must list this information for all active transactions.

Recovery from media failures does not require per-transaction chains of log records. If the server fails due to a media failure, system restart and its log analysis can rebuild the required information in memory. If the server keeps running and its memory state remains intact, active transactions can wait for recovery and then resume or roll back based on in-memory information.

```
T₁: Begin transaction
T₁: Update page 7, slot 9: ...
Database checkpoint
T₁: Update page 4, slot 6: ...
T₂: Begin transaction
T₂: Update page 3, slot 1: ...
Written page 7
T₁: Rollback
T₂: Update page 4, slot 6: ...
T₁: Rollback
T₁: Commit (nothing)
```

Figure 3.2: Alternative to per-transaction log chains.

Figure 3.2 illustrates an alternative to the traditional per-transaction chains of log records. In-memory data structures attached to the transaction manager point to all log records for each transaction. These in-memory pointer arrays are part of the transaction state log in a system checkpoint. If most transactions are shorter than the system checkpoint interval, log volume diminishes because the recovery log contains many fewer LSN values.

Recovery from single-page failures does not require per-transaction chains of log records. Instead, it relies on per-page chains of log records for efficient retrieval of the required log records. For recovery from any single-page failure at any time, a linked list for each database page is required. It is not realistic to keep information equivalent to all per-page linked lists in memory. Thus, for efficient single-page recovery, each log record in the permanent recovery log must include a pointer to the preceding log records pertaining to the same database page, which is equal to the PageLSN value prior to the application of the log record.

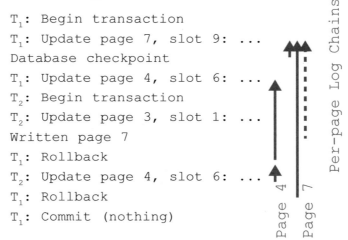

```
T₁: Begin transaction
T₁: Update page 7, slot 9: ...
Database checkpoint
T₁: Update page 4, slot 6: ...
T₂: Begin transaction
T₂: Update page 3, slot 1: ...
Written page 7
T₁: Rollback
T₂: Update page 4, slot 6: ...
T₁: Rollback
T₁: Commit (nothing)
```

Figure 3.3: Per-page chain of log records.

Figure 3.3 illustrates the proposed design. In-memory data structures replace the per-transaction log chains. Instead, per-page chains of log records require an LSN value in each log record modifying a database page. In addition to retracing or replaying the history of each database page, the per-page log chains permit immediate and definitive consistency checks during log replay as well as log archiving.

Taken together, the per-page chain of log records requires additional space in each log record in the permanent recovery log, but a newly proposed in-memory data structure in the transaction manager permits removal of the per-transaction chain of log records and thus can balance the additional space for per-page chains of log records in the persistent recovery log.

## 3.5    SUMMARY OF SINGLE-PAGE RECOVERY

In summary, single-page failures are a new class of database failures in addition to the classic transaction failure, system failure, and media failure. Single-page failures are somewhat like media failures but they do not require replacement media and bulk recovery. Instead, single-page recovery replays the history of individual database pages, starting with earlier correct page images and reversing each single-page history captured in per-page chains of log records in the recovery log.

CHAPTER 4

# Applications of Single-Page Recovery

Single-page recovery is valuable in two kinds of situations: first, by combining it with continuous self-testing and efficient fault detection, it can be a mainstay of self-repairing storage structures; second, by deliberately incurring single-page faults to be repaired later, it can speed up normal transaction processing or provide other benefits. This chapter lists some such situations and cases. All applications and techniques require that the recovery log is on stable storage, i.e., information once logged is never lost.

## 4.1 SELF-REPAIRING INDEXES

Self-repairing indexes [GKS 12] combine efficient (yet comprehensive) detection of single-page faults with immediate single-page recovery. Comprehensive fault detection requires in-page checks as well as cross-page checks. In a self-repairing b-tree index, each node includes low and high fence keys that define the node's maximal permissible key range. Along the left and right edges of the b-tree, these fence keys have values $-\infty$ and $+\infty$, including in the root node. In all other nodes, a node's fence keys equal two keys in the node's parent, i.e., typically branch keys. A node and its leftmost child share the same low fence key value; a node and its rightmost child share the high fence key value. Foster b-trees [GKK 12], which permit local overflow nodes by letting a node be a sibling node's temporary parent, have additional rules for fence keys.

Moreover, for both fault detection and repair, each parent-to-child pointer in a self-repairing b-tree carries an expected PageLSN value for the child page. For simplicity of maintenance, this requires that there be at all times only a single pointer to each page as in Foster b-trees [GKK 12].

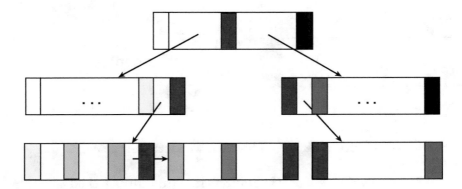

Figure 4.1: Intermediate state in a Foster b-tree.

Figure 4.1 illustrates a foster relationship in a Foster b-tree, i.e., a formerly overflowing node (bottom left) acting as temporary parent node for a newly allocated overflow node (bottom center). Color shades indicate key values; two fence keys delimit each node and its key range. Two system transactions lead to this state. The first one allocates and formats an empty node. Allocation transfers ownership of the page from free space management to the b-tree. Formatting initializes page header and fence records for an empty key range. The second system transaction performs load balancing between foster parent and foster child, which includes adjusting fence keys and the foster key value in the foster parent. The intermediate state shown in Figure 4.1 ends when another system transaction performs an "adoption" operation, moving the parent role, i.e., the child pointer, from the foster parent to the correct permanent parent. In contrast to $B^{link}$-trees [LY 81], a Foster b-tree moves the child pointer rather than copy it, which ensures that there is one pointer per node at all times. A similar intermediate state exists when two nodes underflow and merge.

In a self-repairing b-tree index, the only page without a pointer is the root page. The expected PageLSN value for the root page may be stored in whatever data structure holds the pointer to the root page, e.g., an entry in the database catalogs, or in a separate data structures designed for the purpose, e.g., the "page recovery index" proposed earlier for all database pages [GK 12]. Of course, indexes on the database catalogs as well as the page recovery index may themselves be self-repairing indexes. With a page recovery index per volume, the pointer to the root of the page recovery index belongs into the volume header.

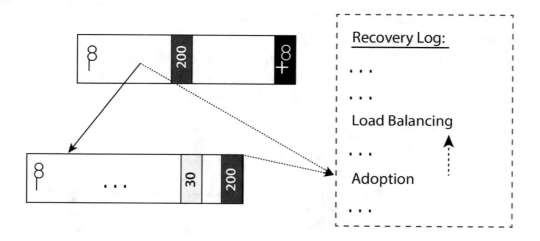

Figure 4.2: Self-repairing b-tree: an expected LSN value with each child pointer.

Figure 4.2 illustrates the additional information required with each child pointer in a self-re-pairing b-tree. The LSN value in the parent, called the expected child LSN (ChildLSN), serves two purposes. First, it permits a consistency check when visiting the child node. If the ChildLSN is older than the child's PageLSN, the parent node needs updating. This update is required when the buffer pool evicts the child page. If the ChildLSN is newer than the child's PageLSN, the child node requires single-page recovery. In both cases, a comprehensive consistency check may traverse the per-page chain of log records in the recovery log from the newer LSN back to the older LSN. Second, if single-page recovery is required, the ChildLSN is the starting point for gathering log records pertinent to the child page and enabling efficient recovery. In a self-repairing Foster b-tree, a temporary or foster parent also carries this information.

## 4.2    WRITE ELISION

Write elision, like partitioned b-trees, can reduce the number of modified pages that must be included in a differential or incremental backup. Partitioned b-trees employed for this purpose concentrate modified index entries in a few partitions such that pages of the master partition remain unchanged and pages of delta partitions each contain many changes. Delta partitions may be merged with each other before or even during differential or incremental backups; master and delta partitions may be merged before or during a full backup. In contrast, write elision reduces the number of modified pages in the persistent database by leaving the database unchanged, relying on log records and single-page recovery to bring a page up-to-date after reading an out-of-date page into the buffer pool.

In write elision, the affected database page (e.g., a b-tree leaf) is in the buffer pool and the update modifies the page image in the buffer pool. For example, during insertion of a new record (e.g., a new b-tree key), the slot number is determined and logged as part of updating the page image. When the buffer pool evicts the modified database page, write elision avoids the effort of writing to the permanent storage device—it deliberately "forgets" to write the dirty buffer pool page to permanent storage. In addition to the efficiency of evicting a dirty page from the buffer pool, the purpose is to keep the database clean in order to reduce the size of incremental backup operations.

Figure 4.3 illustrates a typical situation immediately after write elision in the context of a self-repairing b-tree. The right leaf page (key range 140–200) was dirty but evicted without writing. The ChildLSN in the parent page points to a later log record than the PageLSN value in the leaf page on storage—an oval highlights their difference. Thus, when another thread or transaction follows the path from the parent to the leaf, it will determine that the leaf page is out-of-date. Single-page recovery will quickly bring it up-to-date.

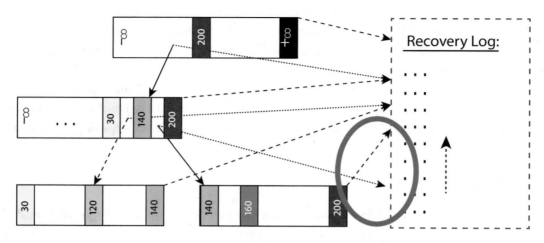

Figure 4.3: Page images, recovery log, and pointers (LSN values) immediately after write elision.

In addition to saving write bandwidth, write elision may benefit system performance in other ways. For example, write elision also promises to reduce costs in append-only storage such as log-structured file systems (e.g., on RAID-4/5/6) and to reduce storage wear-out (e.g., on flash). Even in systems without the "small write penalty" of RAID-4/5/6, write elision can increase transaction throughput where single-page recovery is cheaper than a database write. For example, the recovery log may use flash storage or even non-volatile memory whereas the database uses a traditional disk or disk array.

Write elision may also be useful if the buffer pool must evict a database page containing uncommitted updates, in particular if the "undo" log records for the uncommitted update have not reached stable storage yet. In fact, if restart is to avoid all "undo" actions and if the recovery log is to avoid all "undo" log records, then the buffer pool must not write database pages with uncommitted updates and write elision is a way to evict such database pages from the buffer pool. In other words, write elision becomes an alternative to write-through and write-back.

Yet another possible use for write elision pertains to "time travel" restore after an allocation-only operation, e.g., index creation (see Section 2.7). Since the contents of newly allocated database pages are not logged, new database pages must remain unchanged until copied to the log archive. If a transactional update modifies such a database page, copy-on-write (without de-allocation) or write elision can preserve the original page contents. In this design, correct log archiving requires bypassing the buffer pool holding modified database pages, e.g., index pages with a PageLSN value newer than the commit log record of the index creation with allocation-only logging.

Thus, there are multiple applications for write elision. For any or all of them to be a net positive for system performance or reliability requires suitable governing policies and depends on the specific hardware.

## 4.3   READ ELISION

While write elision may reduce the I/O costs in a system, in particular if the log device is faster than the database storage device, read elision always reduces the I/O costs by delaying an update until the affected database page is in the buffer pool for another purpose, e.g., to answer a query. In its simplest form, read elision works only for insertions, but it can support updates as insertions of replacement records and deletions as insertions of "tomb stone" records.

In read elision, the affected database page is not in the buffer pool and the update is merely logged but not applied until later, which implies some subtle changes in the insertion logic and its log record. For example, in a delayed insertion of a new key into a b-tree node, the slot number remains unknown until the actual insertion. Thus, the log record cannot indicate the slot number as in a standard insertion, including a log record with subsequent write elision. In the case of a Foster b-tree, the initial log record might refer to a foster parent yet eventually the update may apply to a foster child. Update propagation from foster parent to foster child may employ another instance of read elision.

Read elision avoids both the read (into the buffer pool) and the write (back to the database). Maintenance of the database page occurs only when some other operation requires the database page in the buffer pool, e.g., a query. The purpose is to achieve the benefits of buffer trees [A 03] but without the "in-tree" record buffers; instead, the recovery log serves the function of those buffers. An important difference is that buffer trees require buffer space in a parent page, whereas read elision immediately attaches an update to the correct child page, even if only indirectly via the recovery log.

Figure 4.3 also illustrates an update with read elision. The affected leaf page remains unchanged on persistent storage and becomes out-of-date. Up-to-date database contents are only in the recovery log—neither in the buffer pool nor in persistent database storage. Note that the recovery log needs to contain the newly inserted record in any case, e.g., for media recovery.

In most situations, a buffer pool holds all non-leaf pages of all active indexes. In those cases, read elision applies only to the data pages, e.g., the leaf pages of b-tree indexes. In some situations, even a non-leaf page may incur a fault in the buffer pool. In those cases, read elision can still apply: a log record for the insertion is attached to the non-leaf node and its LSN is recorded in that node's parent node. This situation is quite similar to the case of an insertion attached to and logged for a foster parent yet the final insertion goes into a foster child. Thus, Foster b-trees treat foster parents as temporary parent nodes even with respect to read elision.

As read elision defers space allocation in the database, extreme cases may lead to out-of-space errors during read-only queries. Thus, read elision may require integration with free space management. As a final remark on read elision, it is worth pointing out that read elision and, after the deferred update, write elision are orthogonal and can be combined.

## 4.4    DEFERRED "UNDO"

Whereas write elision and read elision apply during normal transaction processing, deferred "undo" is intended for use during media failures, specifically for active transactions with uncommitted updates against failed database media with no replacement media immediately available. In this situation, the traditional method requires that those transactions remain active until they can roll back and apply their "undo" actions against the replacement media, i.e., these transactions are doomed to fail but they cannot fail until media recovery is complete, perhaps many hours later. Deferred "undo" lets these transactions fail and finish immediately, i.e., they log their "undo" actions in spite of the fact that there is no storage to which to apply these action immediately. The advantage of letting these transactions finish is that they can release all their update locks quickly. (A transaction can release its read-only locks immediately when it fails or becomes doomed to fail.)

With deferred "undo," the doomed transactions can log compensation log records without applying them immediately. Instead, media recovery and log replay will discover these log records and apply them when bringing the replacement media up-to-date. Thus, the doomed transactions can finish (after rollback) and can release their locks.

Traditional media recovery cannot let a transaction update the failed media between media failure and completion of media recovery. Thus, there can be no log record pertaining to the failed media in the recovery log and the log archive for that period, and media recovery may skip this period during log replay. In contrast, with deferred "undo," transactions may write log records during that period and media recovery must find and apply them. Thus, it seems that deferred "undo" increases the amount of log to be scanned during log replay in media recovery. If future transactions are able to invoke on-demand single-page repair, however, they can ensure application of "undo" log records by transactions doomed by the media failure.

Deferred "undo" is, of course, related to both read elision and write elision, in both cases specifically for compensation actions. If the relevant database page is still in the buffer pool, despite a failure of the underlying storage media, deferred "undo" is tantamount to write elision. If the relevant database page is not in the buffer pool at the time of a media failure and thereafter, deferred "undo" is equivalent to read elision.

Deferred "undo" differs from write elision and read elision as it relies on logical "undo" rather than physical "redo." An "undo" action may apply to a different database page than the original update. For example, a (user) transaction may modify a b-tree entry in a leaf page, whereupon another (system) transaction splits the leaf and moves the modified b-tree entry to a new leaf page; if the buffer pool evicts both leaf pages and the media fails before the original user transaction commits, its "undo" action must find the correct leaf page.

In general, a deferred "undo" action is logged for the first database page along the root-to-leaf path that is not in the buffer pool. In other words, a ChildLSN value present in the buffer pool can point to the compensation log record. The next access to that child node will find it out-of-date, invoke single-page recovery, and apply the compensation log record. If that child is a branch node rather than leaf node, applying the compensation log record means logging a new compensation log record for the next node along the root-to-leaf path. A foster parent may act like a branch node here and log a new compensation log record for its foster child.

On one hand, media failures do not occur too frequently and it is unclear how valuable deferred "undo" is in practice. On the other hand, when media failure occurs, clearing out active transactions as soon as possible may be a good idea. But then again, instant restore (Chapter 9) may render the entire technique obsolete, but only if replacement media are available immediately.

There is one case of media failures in which deferred "undo" seems indeed useful, namely if a particular device (or its device driver software) repeatedly causes a media failure. A software restart with the particular device not mounted may leave some transaction unable to roll back except with deferred "undo." In general, if the set of mounted devices after a crash may be a subset of those mounted before the crash, deferred "undo" is a useful new technique.

## 4.5    SUMMARY OF SINGLE-PAGE RECOVERY APPLICATIONS

In summary, single-page recovery is a versatile tool for recovery in a variety of situations and applications. These applications of single-page recovery see single-page failures in two contexts: first, increasing robustness for increased reliability and availability of data stores; and second, performance improvements by letting database pages deliberately become out-of-date.

# CHAPTER 5

# Instant Restart after a System Failure

Database system failures and the subsequent recovery disrupt many transactions and entire applications, usually for an extended duration. For those failures, new on-demand "instant" recovery techniques reduce application downtime from minutes or hours to seconds. These new recovery techniques work for databases, file systems, key-value stores, and all other data stores that employ write-ahead logging.

In traditional recovery from a system failure, e.g., a crash of the database server process, applications may resume and start new transactions after recovery has performed the "redo" actions of all log records written since the last checkpoint and then all "undo" (compensation) actions for failed transactions, i.e., those left incomplete at the time of the crash. Both "redo" and "undo" phases may require many random database reads and thus a relatively long time. The design and some implementations of ARIES support new transactions concurrent to the "undo" phase after lock acquisition during the "redo" phase. For even earlier recovery and thus higher application availability, the new, "instant" recovery technique permits new database transactions before any "redo" and "undo" work, imposes little load concurrent to new transactions, and prioritizes recovery of database contents according to the needs of new transactions. Concurrently to "redo" and "undo" recovery guided by new transactions, traditional restart recovery scanning the pre-crash recovery log forward and backward ensures that all recovery actions complete in about the same time as traditional recovery without concurrent new transactions.

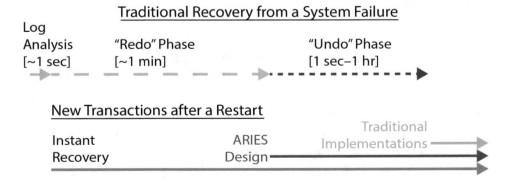

Figure 5.1: Restart phases and new transactions.

The top of Figure 5.1 illustrates the three traditional phases of system recovery and some typical durations. The bottom of Figure 5.1 illustrates application availability after a restart using prior approaches and using the new technique. Top and bottom share a common timeline. The important observation is that previous techniques enable query and transaction processing only after the "redo" recovery phase or even after the "undo" recovery phase, whereas instant recovery permits new queries and update transactions immediately after log analysis. If log analysis takes one second and "redo" and "undo" phases take one minute each, then instant recovery reduces the time from database restart to processing new transactions by about two orders of magnitude compared to both traditional implementations and the ARIES design. Reducing the mean time to repair by two orders of magnitude adds two nines to application availability, e.g., turning a system with 99% availability into one with 99.99% availability.

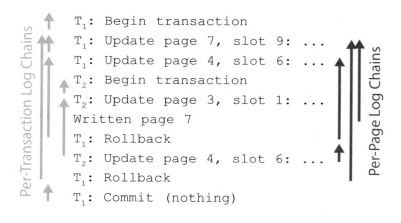

Figure 5.2: Example log contents.

Figure 5.2 introduces a running example with a few log records in a recovery log including the per-transaction log chains (transactions $T_1$ and $T_2$) and the per-page log chains (database pages 4 and 7). Varying from the ARIES design and equal to the design of C-ARIES and D-ARIES, log records describing "undo" (rollback or compensation log records) point to the original "do" log records in order to reduce redundant information in the log. Incidentally, this design permits compensation log records of uniform size and therefore enables accurate pre-allocation of log space for an eventual rollback—with that, a transaction abort cannot fail due to exhausted log space. In the example shown in Figure 5.2, each compensation log record has equal values for the per-transaction pointer and the per-page pointer, with an obvious opportunity for compression. The sequence of log records for page 4, slot 6 implies that transaction $T_1$ released locks incrementally while rolling back. An aborted transaction ends with a commit record after it has "updated back" all its changes in the database. If a transaction ends with no change in the logical database contents, there is no need to force the commit record to stable storage—this applies both to system transactions (see Section 2.8, also discussed below) and to aborted user transactions.

## 5.1    RESTART TECHNIQUES

Immediately upon system restart, instant recovery performs log analysis but invokes neither "redo" nor "undo" recovery. Log analysis gathers information both about pages requiring "redo" and about transactions requiring "undo." Thus, log analysis restores essential server state lost in the system failure, i.e., in transaction manager and lock manager. The buffer pool gathers information about dirty pages. This information does not include images of pages, i.e., random I/O in the database is not required. For efficiency of subsequent recovery, log pages and records should remain in memory after log analysis.

In preparation of "undo" recovery, log analysis tracks the set of active transactions and their locks. It initiates this set from the checkpoint log record. When log analysis is complete, it has identified all transactions active at the time of the crash and their concurrency control requirements. The lock manager holds these locks just as if the transactions were still active. Note that conflict detection is not required during log analysis; the recovery process may rely on successful and correct detection of lock conflicts during transaction processing prior to the crash.

In preparation of "redo" recovery, log analysis produces a list of pages that may require "redo" actions. It initiates this list from the checkpoint log record, specifically the list of dirty pages. Log analysis registers those pages without I/O and thus without page images in memory. In other words, the buffer pool must support allocation of descriptors without page images. While registered for "redo" recovery, a page must remain in the buffer pool. For each such page, the registration includes the expected PageLSN value, i.e., the last log record pertaining to the database page found during log analysis. During log analysis, i.e., the scan over all log records between the last checkpoint and the crash, log records describing page updates (including formatting of newly allocated pages) add or modify registrations of database pages. Log records describing completed write operations un-register the appropriate database page.

Figure 5.3 illustrates the main results of log analysis for the log introduced in Figure 5.2. Dotted pointers show the information acquired during log analysis. For each transaction active at the time of the crash, i.e., only transaction $T_2$, there is a starting pointer for the per-transaction log chain. Figure 5.3 does not show the locks re-acquired during log analysis. For each database page that may have been dirty in the buffer pool at the time of the crash, i.e., pages 3, 4, and 7, there is a starting pointer for the per-page log chain. Page 7 is an interesting special case: log analysis registers it due to the initial update, unregisters it due to the write operation, and registers it again due to the rollback (update back).

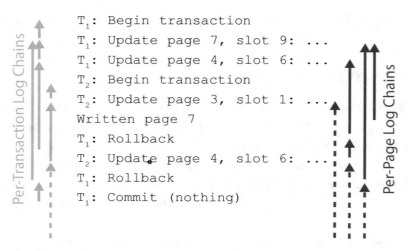

```
T₁: Begin transaction
T₁: Update page 7, slot 9: ...
T₁: Update page 4, slot 6: ...
T₂: Begin transaction
T₂: Update page 3, slot 1: ...
Written page 7
T₁: Rollback
T₂: Update page 4, slot 6: ...
T₁: Rollback
T₁: Commit (nothing)
```

Figure 5.3: Result of log analysis.

After log analysis completes lock re-acquisition and registration of in-doubt database pages in the buffer pool, transaction processing can resume. When an application requires one of the registered pages but the page image in the database is older than the expected PageLSN included in the registration, the buffer pool invokes single-page "redo" recovery. Once single-page "redo" recovery is complete, it rescinds the registration, which prevents future "redo" attempts for this page.

Single-page recovery uses the most recent page image in the database as the backup page. The buffer pool entry includes the most recent log record for the page, i.e., the expected PageLSN. Reversing the per-page chain of log records enables recovery of the page from the most recent available image to its up-to-date state. If the per-page chain of log records includes a log record describing initial formatting of a newly allocated page, the recovery process ignores earlier log records and any earlier page image.

```
T₁: Begin transaction
T₁: Update page 7, slot 9: ...
T₁: Update page 4, slot 6: ...
T₂: Begin transaction
T₂: Update page 3, slot 1: ...
Written page 7
T₁: Rollback
T₂: Update page 4, slot 6: ...
T₁: Rollback
T₁: Commit (nothing)
```

Figure 5.4: On-demand "redo" recovery.

Figure 5.4 illustrates on-demand "redo" recovery based on the information gathered during log analysis and shown in Figure 5.3. This figure shows only those pointers and chains in the recovery log that are required for the example. The example starts with an application requesting page 4 from the buffer pool. Since the buffer pool has this page registered as "in doubt," single-page recovery traverses the per-page chain and invokes the logged "redo" actions. In the rollback (compensation) log record, the per-transaction log chain points to the original log record with the required "undo" information. Some optimizations may apply, e.g., if a compensation log record points to the original log record in both the per-transaction log chain and the per-page log chain, as in Figure 5.4. This situation permits compression in the recovery log as well as skipping some recovery actions during "redo" recovery, somewhat similar to an advanced recovery optimization for ARIES [MP 91].

System transactions require special consideration in recovery. Database locks protect user transactions and their rollback needs, but system transactions do not acquire locks. System transactions merely verify that no locks exist that prevent their intended operation, e.g., removal of a locked ghost record from a b-tree.

System transactions that work on a single database page are the easiest case. A single log record can describe their entire operation. This log record includes or implies transaction commit. Examples include creation or removal of ghost records, reorganization of the indirection vector within a page with ghost slots, changing the size of an individual record by adding or removing ghost space, and defragmentation of free space within a page. By virtue of the single log record for the entire transaction, such system transactions are covered completely by "redo" recovery, including on-demand single-page "redo" as described above.

Multi-page system transactions, e.g., splitting a b-tree node or load balancing among neighbor nodes in a b-tree, may write a single log record or multiple log records. Single-page "redo" recovery covers any system transaction with a single log record. With multiple log records, there may be cases in which one log record is in the recovery log and one is not, due to a system failure. In such cases, both transaction rollback and transaction completion lead to a correct database after recovery, because system transactions do not affect the logical database contents, only their physical representation.

If a system transaction holds its latches until commit, if the buffer pool cannot write a latched page to storage, and if a system crashes before the system transaction commits, then any updates of a failed system transaction cannot be reflected in the database. In other words, recovery may ignore the log records of an incomplete system transaction.

Upon a lock conflict between new and old (pre-crash) transactions, the first question is whether the old transaction has participated in a two-phase commit and is waiting for the global commit decision—in those cases, the new transaction must wait or abort. Otherwise, the old transactions can roll back using standard techniques, i.e., invoking "undo" (compensation) actions and logging them. If transaction rollback touches a database page registered in the buffer pool as requiring "redo" recovery, rollback invokes the appropriate single-page recovery before the transaction rollback resumes. As usual, when a transaction rollback is complete, the transaction writes a log record (it "commits nothing" with no need to force the log record immediately to stable storage), releases its locks, and frees its in-memory data structures.

Figure 5.5 illustrates an example of on-demand "undo" recovery. The example starts with the state shown in Figure 5.4 and an application requesting a lock for page 4, slot 6. This request conflicts with a lock held by pre-crash transaction $T_2$ and therefore triggers "undo" recovery for transaction $T_2$. After rolling back $T_2$'s update of page 4, slot 6, "undo" recovery touches page 3, which triggers single-page "redo" recovery as described earlier and illustrated in Figure 5.4 for page 4. When transaction $T_2$ has been rolled back completely, it is erased from the transaction manager and the new transaction may acquire a lock on page 4, slot 6 without conflict.

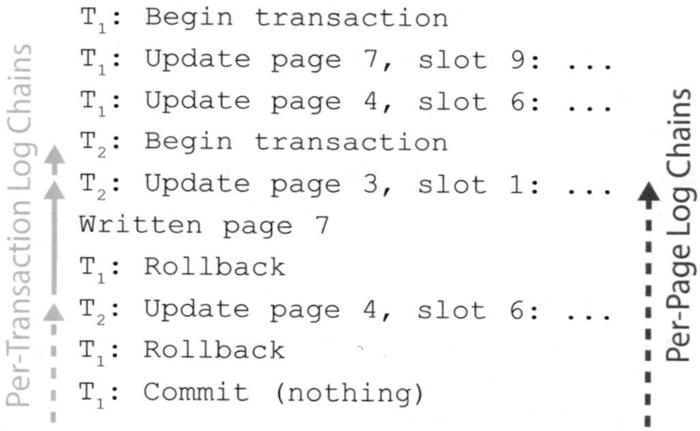

```
              T₁: Begin transaction
              T₁: Update page 7, slot 9: ...
              T₁: Update page 4, slot 6: ...
              T₂: Begin transaction
              T₂: Update page 3, slot 1: ...
              Written page 7
              T₁: Rollback
              T₂: Update page 4, slot 6: ...
              T₁: Rollback
              T₁: Commit (nothing)
```

Figure 5.5: On-demand "undo" recovery.

Just like transaction rollback and "undo" recovery in ARIES, on-demand "undo" recovery logs its actions. Thus, Figure 5.5 only shows the log records consulted in "undo" and "redo" actions after the lock request for page 4, slot 6. After this sequence of actions is complete, i.e., by the time that the lock can be granted, the recovery log has grown to the state shown in Figure 5.6.

Figure 5.6 adds two rollback log records and a commit record to Figure 5.5. Of course, in a restart situation with new transactions, their log records may be interleaved with the rollback log records shown in Figure 5.6. Compared to Figure 5.3, there is no anchor for a per-transaction log chain and only one for a per-page log chain. This is because no incomplete old transaction remains and only page 7 remains in doubt such that it may require on-demand "redo" recovery. The next section considers techniques for efficient recovery of such "lingering" pages.

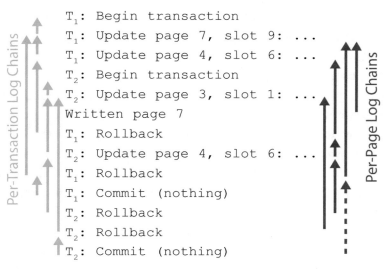

Figure 5.6: Log after on-demand "undo" recovery.

## 5.2 RESTART SCHEDULES

Instant recovery after a system failure differs from traditional recovery, e.g., ARIES techniques, only in the schedule but not in the nature of the recovery actions or in the recovery logic. Instant recovery applies the same "redo" actions and, for each database page, applies them in the same sequence as an ARIES "redo" phase. For each failed transaction, instant recovery applies the same "undo" actions and, for each failed transaction, applies them in the same sequence as an ARIES "undo" phase. Moreover, instant recovery guarantees that for any database page, all required "redo" actions precede any "undo" actions, thus ensuring the same effect as traditional recovery with separate "redo" and "undo" phases. All the schedules below preserve these invariants.

An obvious complement to on-demand recovery focuses on times with idle resources, possibly choosing random in-doubt pages for "redo" recovery and random loser transactions for "undo" recovery. If the recovery logic can predict or anticipate specific usage patterns, it may recover first the appropriate pages and transactions. Otherwise, the pages and transactions may be ordered by their oldest pending log record, i.e., the priority of each page is determined by its oldest log record not yet reflected in permanent storage and the priority of each transaction by its oldest log record. Alternatively, priority for "undo" might be on the transaction with the highest count of log records, i.e., eager "undo" for long transactions and lazy "undo" for short transactions. Other policies may focus on specific devices, volumes, table spaces, catalogs, tables, indexes or index levels, users, applications, etc.

Perhaps the overall simplest single policy gives priority to new transactions and the on-demand recovery required for those transactions, employs idle I/O capacity to load pages into the buffer pool that were resident at the time of the crash, and employs idle CPU capacity to perform "redo" and "undo" recovery.

In addition to various schedules over the continuum from traditional eager recovery to on-demand lazy recovery, combined policies are also possible. In particular, recovery driven by traditional log scans may run concurrently to on-demand incremental recovery. This policy combines the two crucial advantages, i.e., immediate and unrestricted availability of pages and locks for new transactions as well as steady and efficient progress toward completion of all recovery efforts. For example, database page 7 in Figure 5.6 would recover soon after system restart even if no new transaction requests it.

It seems worth pointing out that all alternative schedules require the same total effort. In other words, they modify when recovery occurs for pages and transactions but not how much CPU effort or how much I/O is required altogether. The main difference is that traditional recovery driven by log scans exhibits sequential access in the pre-crash recovery log and random accesses in the database, whereas on-demand recovery requires random (pointer-based) accesses in the recovery log but promises more locality for its accesses to database pages in the buffer pool. In all cases, the relevant parts of the pre-crash recovery log should remain resident in memory after log analysis. As the log records are in memory, log analysis can replace log sequence numbers with virtual memory pointers. Read operations for the most recent page images in the database require random I/O operations in all recovery schedules, in all practical cases one per in-doubt database page. Thus, the total effort is independent of the schedule.

## 5.3   OPTIMIZING LOG SCANS

A traditional restart requires three log scans: a forward log scan for log analysis, a forward log scan for "redo," and a backward log scan for "undo." The first and second forward log scan start with different log records, with the start of the second scan determined only during the first scan (from the checkpoint log record). All three log scans permit further optimizations or substitutes. In fact, these optimizations are independent from and orthogonal to instant restart and on-demand "redo" and "undo."

Log analysis, instead of scanning from the last pre-crash checkpoint to the end of the pre-crash recovery log, may scan backward from the last pre-crash log record toward the last good checkpoint. If the log analysis can simply search for the last good checkpoint, there is no need for depositing its location in a "well-known location," e.g., a small file in the file system, as traditional restart recovery has required for initializing log analysis. Moreover, the separation of winner and loser transactions is simpler and more efficient than in a forward log scan. The first log record encountered for a given transaction decides its fate: if it is a commit log record, the transaction is a winner transaction; otherwise, it is a loser transaction and will require rollback, which implies the need for lock re-acquisition.

Immediate knowledge about the outcome of a pre-crash transaction enables limiting lock re-acquisition to loser transactions. Given that the checkpoint interval is usually much longer than most transactions, most transaction scanned during log analysis are winner transactions. Thus, the backward log scan for log analysis significantly reduces the effort for lock re-acquisition compared to log analysis with lock re-acquisition with a single forward scan of the pre-crash recovery log.

If a loser transaction includes a partial rollback (to a transaction savepoint, e.g., the start of a statement for a transaction specified by a multi-statement script), backward log analysis can easily suspend lock re-acquisition. The first relevant log record encountered during a backward log scan is the last rollback log record of the partial rollback. This rollback log record indicates the log record of the original update. The backward log analysis simply suspends lock re-acquisition between these two log records.

Log analysis with a forward log scan can achieve the same minimal effort for lock re-acquisition by delaying lock re-acquisition into an intermediate phase, e.g., immediately after log scan and log analysis, that focuses on loser transactions and exploits the per-transaction chains of log records. This technique may be less useful for instant restart than for instant failover (Chapter 12).

The "redo" phase may, instead of scanning all log records in the recovery log, scan the buffer pool for database pages registered as "in doubt" and recover those database pages one at a time. Thus, both on-demand "redo" and bulk "redo" can exploit the per-page chains of log records and thus skip over all log records not pertaining to in-doubt database pages. Note that this strategy makes individual database pages available to queries and transactions faster than the "commit_lsn" optimization of ARIES [M 93].

The "undo" phase may, instead of scanning all log records in the recovery log, scan the transaction manager for transactions identified as loser transactions and roll back those transactions one at a time. Thus, both on-demand "undo" and bulk "undo" can exploit the per-transaction chains of log records and thus skip over all log records not pertaining to loser transactions. This strategy may release locks faster than traditional "undo" based on a backward log scan.

The optimizations for "redo" and "undo" rely on log analysis loading and caching the pre-crash log records. With a checkpoint interval (typically a minute) shorter than the buffer pool's retention time for database and log pages (typically five minutes or longer [G 09]), this assumption seems realistic for most database servers. In addition to caching, log analysis may swizzle the pointers representing the per-page and per-transaction chains of log records, limited to loser transactions and in-doubt database pages. Swizzled pointers (replacing LSN values within the pre-crash recovery log buffered in memory during restart) can further speed up page-by-page "redo" and transaction-by-transaction "undo."

Log analysis can acquire locks within indexes only in leaf nodes, i.e., locks on the pages, records, or key values given in a log record. Thus, log analysis can re-acquire all locks required for key-value locking [GK 15, M 90] and key-range locking [G 07, L 93]. If, however, hierarchical locking relies on key values in b-tree branch nodes [G 07], log analysis cannot obtain all relevant key values without inspecting the index structure, which is not advisable during log analysis. Thus, in a system with hierarchical locking within b-tree indexes, log analysis cannot acquire all necessary locks. A possible solution attaches key values requiring locks to the index and migrates such attached deferred locks with the first root-to-leaf traversal, in a way reminiscent of deferred "undo" (Section 4.4). Thus, when a new transaction traverses a b-tree, any deferred lock re-acquisition precedes lock acquisition by the new transaction and lock conflicts force rollback of the old "loser" transaction holding a conflicting lock.

A final optimization recommends a new checkpoint immediately after log analysis and repeatedly during "redo" and "undo" activities. Should another system failure (software crash) interrupt the recovery, these checkpoints reduce the effort and thus time required for the subsequent log analysis and its log scan. In traditional restart with re-acquisition of locks during the "redo" phase, the first checkpoint is possible only after the "redo" phase and thus lock re-acquisition are complete.

## 5.4   SUMMARY OF INSTANT RESTART

In summary, instant restart performs the same recovery actions as traditional restart after a system failure. No additional effort is required, i.e., merely an alternative schedule or two interleaved schedules, in order to provide the appearance of instant recovery and to permit new queries and transactions without restrictions on data selection or on concurrency control techniques.

Table 5.1 summarizes some differences between restarts with the traditional ARIES recovery or with on-demand recovery. The three most important differences are (i) lock re-acquisition during log analysis, (ii) new transactions concurrent to both "redo" and "undo" actions, and (iii) "redo" and "undo" on demand, i.e., triggered and guided by new transactions, their data accesses, and their lock requests. The "redo" and "undo" entries for instant restart focus on on-demand recovery; concurrently to new transactions and to on-demand "redo" and "undo," instant restart permits a background thread driven restart recovery to completion using traditional log scans. A concurrent bulk recovery running in the background may perform "redo" recovery page-by-page or driven by a forward log scan and it may perform "undo" recovery transaction-by-transaction or driven by a backward log scan. The first new checkpoint immediately after log analysis ensures that, if another system failure occurs during restart, it will not re-scan and re-analyze the log records scanned in the first restart attempt. Additional checkpoints during restart recovery can further reduce the work required after another system failure.

| Table 5.1: **ARIES** restart and instant restart | | |
|---|---|---|
| | **ARIES restart** | **Instant restart** |
| Log analysis | Forward log scan | Forward or backward log scan<br>Lock re-acquisition |
| "Redo" | Forward log scan & time-order log replay<br>Lock re-acquisition | Single-page repair for each "in-doubt" page in the buffer pool—on demand and in many independent threads |
| "Undo" | Backward log scan & time-order rollback | Single-transaction rollback of each loser transaction—on demand and in many threads |
| New checkpoint | After "redo" phase | After log analysis |
| New transactions | After "undo" phase or after "redo" phase | After log analysis |
| Concurrent transactions | A lock conflict blocks the new transaction | A lock conflict guides recovery during restart in order to unblock the new transaction |

Even if instant recovery increases the overall duration of recovery (compared to traditional restart without concurrent new transactions), and even if query and transaction processing performance is lower while recovery is not yet complete (compared to transaction processing without any failure and without concurrent recovery), the value of instant restart is the short downtime as perceived by users and applications. In many applications, reducing the time with no transactions is crucial, with substantial impact on business operations and customer satisfaction. Once recovery completes, query and transaction processing performance is the same as after traditional recovery, as shown in Section 15.1.

CHAPTER 6

# Applications of Instant Restart

While instant restart is valuable in its own right, it also enables further extensions and system optimizations.

## 6.1 PARALLEL "REDO" AND "UNDO"

In the context of modern hardware with tens of cores per processor and millions of dirty database pages in a large buffer pool, a single-threaded scan of the pre-crash recovery log may throttle "redo" and "undo" performance. For example, the ARIES design [MHL 92] describes parallel "redo" and "undo" using a single-threaded log scan that partitions pages or transactions to multiple worker threads. The scan bandwidth in the pre-crash recovery log limits both "redo" and "undo" performance.

In contrast, page-by-page "redo" and transaction-by-transaction "undo" can exploit any number of cores and threads, even with a varying degree of parallelism in response to changes in the system load. Each worker thread runs one page at a time and one transaction at a time and when idle chooses the next page or transaction from the buffer pool or the transaction manager. Thus, the alternative designs scanning the buffer pool and the transaction manager seem more suitable for modern hardware.

## 6.2 DISTRIBUTED TRANSACTIONS

In most systems, distributed transactions require a two-phase commit, i.e., two rounds of communication between a commit coordinator and all participants with their local transactions. Some optimizations are common, e.g., all local transactions release their read-only locks in the first phase and read-only local transactions do not participate in the second phase.

In the first phase, each read-write participant guarantees to abide by the global commit decision. Thus, a local transaction in its second commit coordination phase must not fail due to a local reason, e.g., a lock conflict with a high-priority transaction. In other words, such a transaction is in a special protected state.

A local system restart must preserve the protected state and the local transaction's ability to commit or abort according to the global commit decision. A checkpoint log record must list protected transactions or indicate the protected state of uncommitted transactions. Log analysis re-creates the complete list of protected transactions from the checkpoint log record and pre-commit log records in the pre-crash recovery log.

The guarantee to commit or to roll back requires that a protected, undecided transaction must re-acquire its non-read-only locks during system restart. Lock re-acquisition during log analysis is precisely what is needed in order to permit new transactions during "redo" and "undo" even in the presence of protected, undecided local participants of two-phase commit.

While this protected state is required most obviously in the case of two-phase commit, it actually is also required otherwise. Once a transaction has added its commit log record to the in-memory log buffer, no high-priority transaction can preempt it. Even if controlled lock violation [GLK 13] eliminates the lock conflict and thus the need to preempt such a transaction, it still seems best to put such a transaction into a protected state. Put differently, when controlled lock violation weakens a transaction's locks by changing the transaction's state in the transaction manager, this new state must imply protection from preemption.

## 6.3    FAST REBOOT

Sometimes a database server needs rebooting, e.g., for a security patch in the operating system or in the data management software. A large buffer pool may hold many dirty pages and thus a shutdown may take considerable time. For example, a buffer pool of 1 TB holds 125 M pages of 8 KB. If 1% of those are dirty, a shutdown must write 1¼ M dirty pages to storage. A new alternative to flushing those dirty pages relies on restart recovery to bring the affected database pages up-to-date after shutting down the server process without flushing dirty database pages from the buffer pool.

In the past, there was no way around an offline period; either for flushing dirty pages during shutdown or for "redo" recovery during restart. Note that modern machines with larger memory and larger buffer pools make the problem worse, not better. Instant restart eliminates this offline period as it permits new transactions during the repair effort.

With instant restart, the server may simply write a checkpoint and then terminate without flushing dirty pages from the buffer pool. Instant restart and its log analysis are fast as there are no log records after the last pre-reboot checkpoint. New transactions can run immediately after log analysis. There is a performance penalty for a reboot (compared to not rebooting at all), but it does not require an extended offline period. An alternative perspective considers this approach a special case of write elision across a restart. In any perspective, single-page repair enables write elision, instant restart, and thus fast reboot.

## 6.4    SUMMARY OF INSTANT RESTART APPLICATIONS

In summary, the techniques of instant restart enable multiple further extensions and optimizations. In addition to those given above, another application of instant restart is instant failover (Chapter 12).

CHAPTER 7

# Single-Pass Restore

This chapter is about offline restore operations, i.e., restoring database contents lost in a media failure after formatting of a suitable replacement device. Offline recovery assumes a formatted, empty replacement device, starts with recent full, differential, and incremental backups, and includes "redo" of all committed transactions since the last backup and "undo" of any incomplete transactions. Offline recovery does not permit any concurrent transactions against the failed media, even if the system keeps running and executing transactions and queries against data on other volumes.

In this design, the crucial data structure used during restore operations is the log archive. In particular, the recovery log is crucial for transaction commit, transaction rollback, and recovery from a system failure (crash), whereas the log archive primarily serves media failures. Single-page recovery may use both the recovery log (for recent log records) and the log archive (for older log records). The discussion within this chapter focuses on the log archive and recovery from media failures; Chapter 9 focuses on instant restore and its use of single-page recovery as part of media recovery.

Multiple examples below assume the following sizes, chosen for easy calculations as well as a resemblance of realism: each database storage device of 4 TB is ¾ full with a sustained access rate of 300/s and a sustained transfer bandwidth of 300 MB/s, a daily incremental backup of 1% of all allocated database pages or 30 GB, and a daily log volume of 3% thereof or about 1 GB. These numbers imply a full backup of 3 TB (ignoring compression), a backup time of 10,000 seconds or 3 hours, a differential backup that grows over the course of a week from 1% to 6% (i.e., from 30 GB to 180 GB, or from 100 seconds to 600 seconds, or from 2 minutes to 10 minutes). They also imply about 40 updates per log page (e.g., log records of 200 bytes in pages of 8 KB), and logging and log archiving bandwidth of 12 KB/s. Note that the calculated logging and log archiving bandwidth refers to a single storage device, with system bandwidth higher by the count of storage devices; that it represents an average, with peak bandwidths typically much higher; and that logging devices are chosen and operated optimized for latency, not bandwidth. A database server of moderate size in a busy period might try to log 4 MB/s in 500 log pages of 8 KB. Traditional logging on a mirrored disk may achieve this performance by writing multiple log pages in each I/O operation. The examples using these values enable back-of-the-envelope estimates and readers are invited to substitute other values and assumptions.

## 7.1   PARTIALLY SORTED LOG ARCHIVE

The essence of restoring a database volume to an up-to-date state in a single pass is the order of database pages and of log records. For the backup and replacement media, the ideal order proceeds by page identifier, from the lowest to the highest, i.e., a single sequential pass over backup and replacement media. The problem is that the recovery log is written in the order of time or of LSN values, not in the order of database pages.

Once the set of required log records is known, i.e., log records selected for the failed device and for the appropriate time interval, those log records could be sorted by database page identifier. Typically, this would require a multi-pass external merge sort, i.e., run generation with run sizes limited by the memory allocation dedicated to the restore operation followed by a merge step or, in extreme cases, multiple merges steps. This is the design implied by Gray [G 78] and mentioned in Section 2.5. Moreover, since the required time range in the log is known only after a failure has occurred, the multi-pass sort logic can run only after the failure. It thus adds to the media recovery time. In contrast, the desired combination of features is continuous log archiving during transaction processing and log archiving logic that starts immediately after replacement media are available and then requires only a single pass over backup, log archive, and replacement media.

The crucial new technique that enables single-pass continuous log archiving as well as immediate single-pass up-to-date restore operations is to sort log records during archiving, yet to divide the logic of external merge sort between log archiving and restore operation. The obvious way to divide this logic is to separate run generation and merging. In other words, log archiving not only suppresses some log records and compresses the remaining ones but also sorts log records into runs. Each run in the log archive captures a time interval in the original recovery log, i.e., a continuous range of LSN values. Within each run, however, log records are sorted by the page identifier with the database.

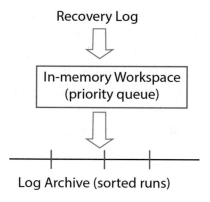

Figure 7.1: Runs of log records sorted by database page.

Figure 7.1 illustrates log archiving, i.e., copying log records from a recovery to a log archive, with log records in the former sorted entirely by time (LSN values) and log records in the latter partitioned into time intervals and, within each time interval, sorted by database page identifier.

In the example introduced earlier, each database storage device requires sort logic for 12 KB/s, truly a minor additional load during transaction processing, even if each database node in a cluster processes data, updates, log records, etc. for two dozen storage devices.

When compared to a fully sorted log archive, the crucial advantage of a partially sorted log archive is the efficiency in its creation. Creation of a partially sorted log archive is akin to run generation in an external merge sort. Thus, log archiving writes each log record to storage only once, the final log archive. Of course, due to in-memory sorting and run generation, archiving writes log records not immediately but after a short delay for in-memory processing. In contrast, creation of a fully sorted log archive requires multiple passes over the log records, e.g., run generation and final merge step.

When compared to a traditional, unsorted log archive, the crucial advantage of a partially sorted log archive is the efficiency in its use, i.e., during a restore operation. Replaying the log records in an unsorted log archive requires many random accesses in the replacement database. In contrast, a single merge step can merge many runs from a partially sorted log archive. The merge logic may pipeline the log records into the restore logic without intermediate files.

Of course, for extremely large log archives with an extremely large number of runs, an intermediate merge step may be required. However, such a merge step may run independently of the archiving logic and of the restore logic, e.g., once a day during a period of low database activity. Altogether, the important advantage of a partially sorted log archive is that both log archiving and restore operations each remains a single-pass algorithm (in terms of I/O), essentially employing the logic of run generation and merging of an external merge sort.

## 7.2    ARCHIVING LOGIC

Steady-state transaction processing writes log records to the traditional recovery log on "stable storage." After a page filled with log records is safely on stable storage, an in-memory sort operation may consume the log records and, sorted by page identifier, write them to the log archive. Only log records already in the recovery log may go to the log archive; otherwise, the logic for restarting log archiving after a system crash becomes unnecessarily complex.

In this design, log archiving is a continuous activity. Thus, memory allocation and CPU effort for sorting log records and adding them to the log archive are required as continuous system load in addition to transaction and query processing. The memory allocation may be moderate, perhaps 1 GB in a large server and less in a small server or any server with moderate or small load. A promising memory allocation equals 5–10 minutes worth of log records, thus producing 150–300 log archive partitions per day. In the running example introduced above, the daily log volume is 1 GB or about 7 MB in 10 minutes, calling for a sort workspace of about 5–10 MB. $10^5$ log records in the sort workspace require about 17 comparisons or perhaps 1,000 CPU cycles per log record. Sorting $10^7$ log records per day requires $10^{10}$ CPU cycles or a few CPU seconds per day.

Log archiving sorts eligible log records by volume and page identifiers such that, within each run or partition of the log archive, log records are clustered and sorted first by volume, then by page identifier, and finally by the original LSN of the log records. Thus, if a single device fails, recovery from the log archive may be faster than by a traditional log replay if for no other reason than clustering of log records for the failed device.

While replacement selection has advantages for run generation in many situations, particularly due to run sizes expected to be twice the memory allocation, in the case of log archiving it is more important to maintain a simple mapping between time interval (i.e., position in the original log) and run (i.e., partition in the log archive). A simple mapping greatly simplifies restart of log archiving after a system failure. In addition to larger runs, replacement selection consumes its input and produces its output more continuously than, for example, run generation by quicksort with its cycles of read, sort, and write phases. Fortunately, a priority queue and continuous input and output can be used in log archiving, but without the logic that includes late input items in the current output run. Thus, run size (i.e., partition size in the log archive) equals the memory allocation during run generation, perhaps with some moderate loss due to variable-size records [LG 98].

In a normal start-up, i.e., after a clean shutdown with the recovery log ending with a checkpoint listing no active transactions and no dirty pages in the buffer pool, log archiving fills its workspace with log records already written to the recovery and thus archiving begins a little later than transaction processing. In a clean shutdown, after all transactions are finished, all dirty pages written from the buffer pool, and all log records written to the recovery, log archiving sorts the log records remaining in its workspace and writes them to the log archive. Thus, log archiving lags a little both during start-up and shutdown.

In a system crash, some log records remain unwritten to both recovery log and log archive, some log records are in the recovery log but not the log archive, and most log records are in both recovery log and log archive. Either the log analysis phase or a new phase immediately before or after log analysis must ensure equal contents in recovery log and log archive by copying the appropriate log records from the recovery log to the log archive. Doing so simplifies "redo" recovery and single-page recovery by permitting them to rely entirely on the log archive. Obviously, this step also sorts log records on page identifiers. It finishes the most recent run in the log archive and starts the next one.

A traditional log archive is merely a copy of the recovery log, perhaps compressed. An alternative perspective regards the recovery log as the history of the server and its transactions and the log archive as the history of the database. This distinction guides what information is truly required in a log archive. For example, the history of the server is not required for database restore operations; thus, the log archive has no need for checkpoint log records or log records of successful write operations.

Log archiving suppresses and compresses log records as much as possible, but also extends each log record by its original LSN value. Thus, while each original log record contains LSN values for the preceding log records of the same transaction and for the same database page, log records in the partially sorted log archive contain the PageLSN values of the affected database page before and after application of the log record. Of course, similar LSN values can be compressed, e.g., by representing one as a difference from the other.

In fact, the information transfer from the recovery log to the log archive really is rewriting history: while the recovery log is a history of individual update transactions and of the server (e.g., checkpoints), the log archive is a history of the database. Thus, individual transactions no longer matter, and only their effects on the database matter. Consequently, the "net change" calculation also suppresses transaction identifiers within log records, other transaction information, e.g., transaction begin and commit, and log records about server state, e.g., database checkpoints or successful write operations. With that, the "net change" calculations here supersede "restricted repeating of history" in ARIES/RRH [MP 91].

Moreover, all "redo" information for a page may be aggregated in a "net change" calculation. Several examples suggest themselves: a "do" and "undo" operation (an original log record and its compensation log record) may be suppressed entirely. An insertion and subsequent deletion may be combined into nothing or into insertion of a ghost key. A deletion and subsequent insertion may be combined to an update. Finally, multiple insertions may be aggregated into a single multi-record insertion.

## 7.3     RESTORE LOGIC

The offline restore logic using the log archive is surprisingly simple and, importantly, proceeds in a single pass that writes the replacement database and reads all backups and the log archive. Before the restore logic may proceed, however, transactions accessing the failed media must abort and log records lingering in the archiving workspace must be flushed to the log archive (or at least its in-memory workspace). As transactions roll back, they attempt to "update back" their original changes and log their actions in compensation log records; due to the media failure, however, they cannot update the media but they must nonetheless produce the log records and both recovery log and log archive require them. As the buffer pool cannot write dirty pages back to the failed media, the restore operation will determine their correct up-to-date contents and restore them.

The restore operation first merges the most recent full backup, the differential backup if one exists, and any existing incremental backups. More precisely, the restore logic proceeds page by page and, for each page, selects the most recent page image from the backups. From the log archive and its partitions, which are log records sorted by device identifier and then by page identifier, the merge logic reassembles the page history and then computes the up-to-date page image, writes it to the replacement device, and proceeds to the next page. The log records pertaining to a database page must form a contiguous list of timestamps with their before- and after-update PageLSN values. This list must begin with the PageLSN value found in the most recent page image from the backups.

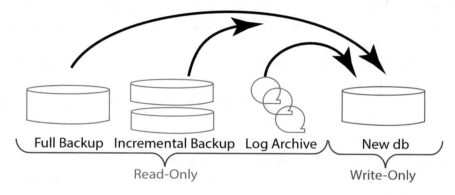

Figure 7.2: Merging backups and partitions in the log archive.

Figure 7.2 illustrates a restore situation with a full backup, two incremental backups, and a log archive with three partitions. The I/O pattern is that of the final pass of a merge sort, even if the logic is a slight variation: it selects the most recent one among page images in the backups and it assembles a contiguous page history from the log records in the log archive.

The number of backups is typically very small: one full backup, possibly one differential backup, and a few incremental backups since the last full or differential backup. The number of partitions in the log archive might be substantial, however. For example, if the sort workspace allocated to log archiving holds only 5 minutes worth of log records, log archiving produces 12 partitions per hour, almost 300 partitions per day, about 2,000 partitions per week, or nearly 10,000 partitions per month. Media recovery can succeed with a single merge step only if it can merge all partitions at once, with sufficient buffer space for each. With backups and log archive prime candidates for low-cost high-capacity storage, i.e., traditional disk drives or arrays, the buffer space should be ½ MB per partition. If the most recent backup is one week old, this require a merge fan-in of about 2,000 and thus about 1 GB including a few extra buffers for prefetching guided by forecasting.

If a single merge step is not possible with such a large fan-in, intermediate merge steps are required. These can be asynchronous to both log archiving and restore operations. In other words, they may lag log archiving but they should be sufficiently frequent and fast to enable recovery at any time with a feasible merge fan-in. For example, a daily merge of 300 partitions may use only

150 MB of memory yet enable single-pass media recovery at any time, with a merge fan-in of about 300 (including the current day) and even with only one monthly backup. With respect to the effort for intermediate merge steps, note that the log archive and its partitions are much smaller than the database and traditional daily incremental backups.

## 7.4     ACTIVE TRANSACTIONS

Single-pass restore, as mentioned earlier, is an offline operation. In other words, while a single-pass merge of backup and log archive populates the replacement device, no active transactions may query or update the device contents. Instant restore (Chapter 9) removes this limitation. However, in the absence of instant restore, what is the fate of active transactions during single-pass restore of a device? In other words, if a transaction has, at the time of a media failure, already queried or updated the failed contents, how does this transaction resume or roll back?

A read-only transaction can readily abort without any need for rollback actions on the failed device. Alternatively, it can pause until restore operations finish and then resume. Similarly, an update transaction can pause and resume later. The problem with any paused transaction is, however, that it retains its locks, including those locking data on other devices.

An incomplete transaction cannot commit or roll back in the ordinary way. It may commit eventually (after the restore operation) if the existing log records indeed guarantee durability, i.e., single-pass restore will include all updates already logged by the transaction. It may commit earlier if no further updates are required on the failed device. On the other hand, an incomplete transaction cannot roll back if its "undo" actions conflict with the offline restore operation.

Some techniques discussed earlier as applications of single-page recovery provide some relief. An incomplete transaction may roll back with deferred "undo" (Section 4.4), i.e., it produces rollback log records into the recovery log but it does not apply these rollback log records to database pages. Instead of transaction abort, an incomplete transaction may also continue with "read" elision (Section 4.3) or with write elision (Section 4.2). Write elision applies only if the required database pages are resident in the buffer pool and if the restore operation relies on database pages in the buffer pool rather than those derived from backup and log archive. Read elision requires a unique path to the data such that any subsequent query or update operation will detect incomplete update propagation. For example, if the root page of a self-repairing b-tree (Section 4.1) resides on a different device, a transaction may write a log record for an insertion and modify the root node such that the first access will find its child page out-of-date. Eventually, single-page recovery can propagate the insertion toward and eventually to the appropriate leaf page. Depending on the self-repairing properties of the root page, e.g., expected LSN values in the index catalog, read elision may apply even to the index root page, i.e., to cases in which an entire index resides on the failed device.

## 7.5    SUMMARY OF SINGLE-PASS RESTORE

In summary, a partially sorted log archive offers both fast, continuous log archiving and fast, single-pass restore. Archiving remains a single pass over the log records, comparable to traditional log archiving that merely suppresses some log records and some log record fields, and then compresses log records. The new archiving logic is quite similar to run generation in an external merge sort.

Log replay, i.e., taking a database image forward through time, merely needs to merge a database backup and the log archive. The new restore logic is quite similar to the final merge step in an external merge sort. Reading the database backup and writing the new up-to-date database both proceed with the bandwidth of the respective I/O devices. The restored database is immediately up-to-date. In traditional restore operations, log replay takes by far the most time due to many random I/O operations in the restored database. In contrast, the new restore logic hides log replay within the phase restoring a full backup without substantially increasing the time required. In addition, it can hide comprehensive in-stream consistency checks for the new database as described below for virtual backups (Section 8.3).

Table 7.1: ARIES restore and single-pass restore

|  | **ARIES Restore** | **Single-pass Restore** |
|---|---|---|
| Transaction logging | Same techniques and costs | |
| Database backups | Offline or online full, differential, or incremental backups | Offline or online full backups |
| Log archiving | Copy and compress original recovery log | Partial sort + aggregation of log records |
| Restoring backups | One backup at a time; merge possible | Merge backup and runs of the log archive—random I/O with large transfers as in external merge sort |
| Log replay | In order of original execution—much random page I/O in the database | |
| Active transactions | Suspended during restore, rollback after restore is complete | |
| New transactions | Only after restore is complete | |

Table 7.1 compares traditional ARIES media restore and single-pass restore. There is no difference for user transactions, system transaction, and their logging activities. While ARIES requires full backups and benefits from differential and incremental backups, despite their complexity and run-time effort, single-pass restore renders differential and incremental backups obsolete (Section 8.4) and permits taking full backups without imposing any load on the database server (Section 8.3). Log archiving differs substantially: ARIES-based systems merely copy and perhaps compress log records whereas single-pass restore requires partial sorting, i.e., run generation, during

log archiving. Like sort-based aggregation in query execution, partial sorting aids aggregation of log records, quite similar to early duplicate removal in sorting [BD 83]. The restore process, when invoked, also differs substantially: ARIES-based systems first restore one or multiple backups, possibly merging a full backup, a differential backup, and one or multiple incremental backups, and then reply the log, possibly after sorting the log records for "fast log apply" [S 05]. In contrast, single-pass restore merges all available backups and the runs of the log archive in a single merge step, thus restoring fully up-to-date database pages on the replacement device. Both approaches restore offline, i.e., active transactions with uncommitted updates on the failed device as well as new queries and transactions against the replacement device all must wait until the restore operation complete. Instant restore (Chapter 9) removes this offline period.

CHAPTER 8

# Applications of Single-Pass Restore

The essence of single-pass restore is the partially sorted log archive, created with a single-pass algorithm embedded in the archiving logic and used with a single-pass algorithm that merges backups and partitions in the log archive. The partially sorted log archive enables functionality beyond efficient log archiving and efficient restore operations. For example, it renders all differential and incremental backups obsolete and it permits backup commands that complete in seconds rather than hours.

## 8.1 PIPELINE EXTENSIONS

A simple and obvious extension of single-pass restore immediately creates a new, up-to-date full backup. Should another media failure occur in the future, recovery can start with this new backup. Thus, creation of such a backup renders all earlier log records in the log archive obsolete. Creation of a new, up-to-date backup requires extending the pipeline that creates an up-to-date replacement database with one or two additional steps. The last step writes the new backup; the optional preceding step may suppress white space and apply any other desired form of compression.

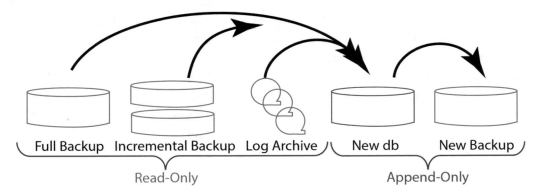

Figure 8.1: Single-pass restore with immediate backup.

Figure 8.1 illustrates a backup file created as a side effect of an single-pass restore operation. Beyond the logic to restore the new database, the recovery logic compresses the page images (using the same techniques as for other backups, e.g., suppression of white space) and appends them to the backup media.

The sequential pass reading the old backup and writing both the replacement database and the new backup enables in-stream consistency checks for all three. Obviously, the consistency checks for the replacement database and new backup are more important than for the old backup, but if the replacement database or new backup fails the consistency check, it is useful to know whether the inconsistency stems from the old backup or from the log archive. For example, if the backup is inconsistent but the log archive is good, another recovery attempt can start with an older backup. A consistency check within the recovery pipeline matches facts derived repeatedly from a database, and an aggregation algorithm or bit vector filtering can determine the required number of occurrences of matching facts [GS 09]. For example, the fact "page 47 belongs to b-tree index 11, it is a leaf (level-0) node with key range (fence keys) x and y" can be extracted from both page 47 and its parent (level-1) page in the index. It must be found precisely twice in any database scan. Similar matching facts apply to the relationships between secondary indexes and their table's primary data structure. Checks between tables with a foreign key integrity constraint require traditional bit vector filters, as do materialized views and their relationships to their base tables. Suitable filters in a restore pipeline from an old backup to a new backup can extract and verify such facts with minimal additional overhead. The facts to match and the complexity of the matching logic depend on the index structure, e.g., b-tree versus hash table or, among alternative b-tree structures, $B^{link}$-tree [LY 81] vs. Foster b-tree [GKK 12].

Between log replay and writing to the replacement database and the backup, the restore logic can also optimize database pages. For example, within each database page, it can defragment in-page free space, remove ghost (invalid) records, compress valid records, etc. It can also move database page, e.g., defragment leaf pages of a b-tree for faster sequential scans. While all affected index pages are in the database pool, the restore logic can apply load balancing or other structural change such as adoption in Foster b-trees [GKK 12]. For the database, there is little difference whether such database reorganization steps run part of the restore logic or run later. If an immediate backup is part of the restore pipeline, however, the place of the reorganization step determines whether the backup reflects database pages before or after the reorganization.

## 8.2    INSTANT BACKUP

Among the most onerous database maintenance tasks are backups, due to large data volumes, long durations, and their impact on system load and, in the case of remote backup storage, network load. For large databases on large devices, backups can take hours simply for reading all allocated database pages and for writing them to the backup media. Instant backup reduces the duration of backup commands from many hours to seconds or minutes.

Clearly, it is not possible to perform a traditional backup operation in seconds or to write a full backup file in minutes. In other words, an instant backup must rely, at least in part, on pre-existing data. The crucial idea is to combine a pre-existing backup with a log archive in such a way that these files together provide the benefits of a backup taken at the time of the backup command. Thus, this technique redefines what constitutes a backup, focusing not on a single file but on guaranteed efficient restore operations instead.

Usage of these files is precisely as in a single-pass restore operation, i.e., a high-speed merge of an old backup with partitions of the log archive. This merge operation may occur immediately as part of the backup command, asynchronously after the backup command is completed, or lazily during a restore operation. The last option is correct but, in the case of excessively many partitions in the log archive, it increases the restore time after a media failure. Sufficient merging should happen immediately or asynchronously to ensure that a restore operation requires only a single merge step.

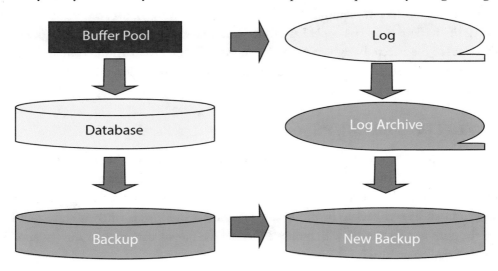

Figure 8.2: Instant backup.

Figure 8.2 illustrates data flow in transaction processing, database backup, log archiving, instant backup, and single-pass restore. It is, of course, quite similar to Figure 2.1, except that the combination of out-of-date backup and log archive produces a new backup rather than a replacement database. During transaction processing, the database system writes log records to the recovery log and dirty pages to the database. Database backups, once created, remain read-only and fall out-of-date. Log archiving sorts log records from the recovery log into runs and perhaps even indexes these records using a partitioned b-tree on page identifier (run number equal partition identifier). When a restore operation is needed, a single-pass restore operation merges an out-of-date database backup and the appropriate partitions in the log archive, with only moderately more I/O than copying a backup to new database media. When a new backup is wanted, the most recent backup and the appropriate partitions in the log archive are immediately ready yet, when needed, they can serve the purpose of a traditional backup.

An instant backup defines a backup point similar to that of an offline backup (see Section 2.4). Such points occur regularly during log archiving into a partially sorted log archive, namely when the archiving logic switches from one output partition to the next. In the case of an explicit backup command, the archiving logic can force such a switch immediately by assigning the log record currently scanned and all subsequent log records to a new output partition. As soon as this switch point has worked through the run generation logic, e.g., the priority queue, the instant backup is complete in the form of pre-existing backup file and a fixed set of partitions in the log archive.

For even faster completion of an explicit backup command, the switch from one log archive partition to a new one is not required. A restore operation, however, must scan the entire partition containing the backup time and apply log records selectively, depending on the state (and the PageLSN value) of the affected database pages. Moreover, a log archive partition containing a backup time must inhibit aggregation of log records, because a restore operation might find any database page in any intermediate state.

## 8.3    VIRTUAL BACKUPS

A virtual backup operation produces an up-to-date backup image of the database without even accessing the database. In other words, it is not a backup at all in the sense that it does not read any information from the active database; nonetheless, it produces a backup image just as if it had. It differs from an instant backup by producing a single backup image, whereas an instant backup satisfies the purpose of a backup with multiple files, i.e., an out-of-date backup and the appropriate partitions of the log archive.

The basic idea of virtual backups does not require any new techniques: take an old backup and replay the recovery log in order to produce not an up-to-date database image but an up-to-date backup image. In the past, however, this process would require completely sorting the recovery log covering days or weeks or it would require decompressing the old backup onto standard database storage followed by log replay with hours or days of random I/O operations.

With an older backup and a partially sorted log archive, a virtual backup can be simple and fast. The operation merely merges the older backup and the partitions of the log archive, very similarly to a single-pass restore operation. The difference, if any, is the precise format of the produced backup. For example, while a restore operation writes page images on page boundaries in the target space, a backup operation may compress page contents, suppress empty space within pages (often >25% in b-tree pages), etc.

A virtual backup operation may produce a backup image with incomplete transactions, just as an online backup operation does. While using this backup image, transactions must continue (with subsequent log records) or they must roll back.

A special optimization enabled by efficient virtual backup operations involves two nodes and minimizes the required network bandwidth between them. Consider a primary node with the database and the recovery log as well as a secondary node with backup images and the log archive. During normal transaction processing, the primary node ships a copy of its local log, perhaps with some log records removed such as checkpoint log records, to the secondary node, where the log archiving logic sorts and compresses the log records to form the log archive. When it is time to take a new backup, traditional backup operations require substantial additional network bandwidth from the primary to the secondary nodes. The provisioned hardware must satisfy this bandwidth requirement even if this bandwidth is useful only during backup operations. The virtual backup operation can run entirely within the secondary node, with no network bandwidth needs for page images, simply by merging an earlier backup with the partitions of the log archive, both local to the secondary node. Thus, the proposed remote virtual backup technique reduces bursts in the load of primary node and of the network, permitting to provision both for the transaction processing workload rather than for additional bursts due to backup operations.

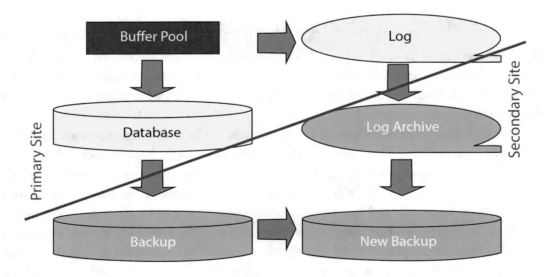

Figure 8.3: Remote log archiving and remote virtual backup.

Figure 8.3 illustrates information flow and in particular node assignment of backup operations in a remote virtual backup. The primary node is in the top-left and the secondary node is in the bottom-right. The primary node performs user transactions against its database, writing appropriate log records to the local recovery log. It also ships log records to the secondary node, where the archiving logic sorts and compresses the log records into a partially sorted log archive. If the number of runs in the log archive approaches the threshold for a single merge step, the secondary node also merges runs. Alternatively, it may merge runs regularly and proactively, e.g., once a day. The secondary node also holds backup copies of the database, which, once created, remain read-only and thus fall out-of-date. When it is time to create a new backup file, the secondary node merges an out-of-date backup and the runs of the log archive, typically in a single merge step. Merging with large units of I/O is almost as efficient as sequential I/O. In other words, the required I/O effort is equal to reading the old backup once and sequentially, reading the log archive once and almost as fast as sequentially, and writing the new backup once and sequentially.

In addition to full backups, virtual backup operations can also produce differential and incremental backup images. Instead of copying unmodified database pages from the old backup to the new one, only modified pages are copied, with the originals taken from a full, differential, or incremental backup. If all differential and incremental backups are derived from older backups rather than the database, there is no need for special data structures (bitmaps) in the database in order to track recently changed database pages (see Section 2.4).

## 8.4    OBSOLETE INCREMENTAL BACKUPS

Even if differential and incremental backups may become simpler and perhaps even more efficient to obtain, they actually become obsolete. Since log replay is as simple and efficient as a merge operation between full backup and log archive, there seems to be little advantage in producing and using differential and incremental backups.

The traditional value of differential and incremental backups has been to shorten log replay with its numerous random I/O operations in the database. Moreover, a database page with multiple updates during a single day (interval between incremental backups) requires only a single restore operation rather than multiple individual "redo" operations in traditional log replay, possibly with eviction from the buffer pool and thus repeated random I/O operations for the same database page.

With log replay based on merging partitions of a partially sorted log archive, and thus a stream of log records completely sorted on page identifiers just like a database backup, these arguments are obsolete. First, a restore operation reads (from the old backup) and writes (to the new backup or the replacement database) each database page only once. Second, the I/O patterns are sequential in the old backup, in the new backup or in the replacement database, and within each partition of the log archive. Even if dozens of partitions are required from the log archive, the I/O units can be such that I/O bandwidth resembles sequential I/O more than random I/O. Third, due to sorting, log archiving can aggregate multiple log records pertaining to the same database page.

Thus, each aggregated log record in the log archive represents a net change for the affected database pages. Individual original log records are required only for periods during which an online backup was taken from the database. In summary, the new substitute for log replay, i.e., merging backup and log archive, is faster than differential and incremental backups plus traditional log replay.

## 8.5    SUMMARY OF SINGLE-PASS RESTORE APPLICATIONS

In summary, a partially sorted log archive enables continuous, single-pass creation of the log archive from the recovery log as well as single-pass log replay by merging backups and sorted runs from the log archive. Without substantially increasing the complexity of log archiving, log replay becomes so efficient that it can supplant differential and incremental backups. Since a simple merge operation can produce an up-to-date full backup, it can be more efficient to create a new, up-to-date full backup from an old backup and the log archive than to scan the active database and to interfere with active transaction processing. Finally, the continuous process of log archiving can switch to a new output run at any time; forcing this switch quickly produces a set of files that together enable efficient media recovery and thus may take the place of an up-to-date full backup.

CHAPTER 9

# Instant Restore after a Media Failure

Obviously, it is impossible to finish a restore operation much faster than single-pass restore does. Therefore, "instant restore" merely gives the illusion of a truly instant restore operation: it permits queries and updates practically immediately after a replacement device is available, i.e., formatted but empty. Nonetheless, in spite of concurrent transactions, the restore operation may complete in about the same time as an offline single-pass restore operation, i.e., much faster than a traditional restore operation with log replay using log records in their original order.

## 9.1 INDEXED BACKUP AND LOG ARCHIVE

The principal technique enabling the appearance of an instant restore operation is on-demand restore operations for the immediately needed pieces of the failed media. In other words, the failed media and its replacement are conceptually divided into segments (a page or a set of contiguous pages), and each time a transaction attempts to access one of those segments for the first time after the failure, that particular segment is recovered from the most recent backup and from the log archive.

In order to enable efficient on-demand single-segment media recovery, both the backup and the log archive require appropriate indexes. A full backup does not require an index if a database page identifier implies a byte offset in the backup file, i.e., if the backup logic fails to copy only allocated pages, to eliminate free space within pages, and to forgo other opportunities for compression. In the indexes for the backups, each index entry maps a segment, e.g., a database page identifier, to a location in the backup file. A large device might be broken into 1 M segments and therefore the index requires up to 1 M entries. In the running example of Chapter 7, a database storage device of 4 TB may be broken into 1 M segments of 4 MB.

A database page identifier is a "natural" sort key for a backup file; thus, it is simple and efficient to build a suitable b-tree index. A partially sorted log archive similarly permits efficient creation of a b-tree index, albeit a partitioned b-tree. In the log archive organized as a partitioned b-tree, each index entry is a log record. The run number is the partition identifier and thus prefixes the sort key. Thus, the complete sort key in each log record within this index consists of partition identifier, device and page identifiers, and finally and LSN value, e.g., the PageLSN before or after application of the log record to the affected database page.

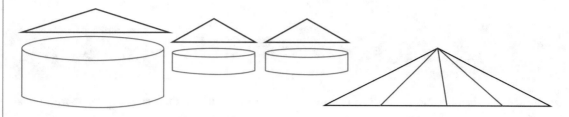

Figure 9.1: Database backups and log archive with indexes.

Figure 9.1 illustrates a full backup, two incremental backups, and a log archive. Each of them is sorted and indexed on database page identifiers. The indexes on the backup files are traditional b-tree indexes. The index on the log archive is a partitioned b-tree, with a b-tree partition for each run in the partially sorted log archive. For any database page, the backups permit quick retrieval of all backup images (even if only the most recent page image is required for recovery); and the partitioned index on the log archive permits quick retrieval of all log records pertaining to a single database page or to all database pages within a segment.

In addition to the partitioned b-tree, a bit vector filter might speed up search for log records pertaining to a specific database page or segment within a storage device. With the bit vector filter, a search for log records for a specific database page or segment may skip over partitions in the log archive guaranteed not to include log records for that database page or segment.

Instead of a partitioned b-tree, any data structure will do that can map a partition in the log archive plus a segment identifier within the database to a byte offset within the log archive. For example, if each partition in the log archive is a file, a fixed set of values in the first bytes of the file can point to appropriate locations within the file. This alternative design exploits the file system to manage partitions within the log archive and the fixed set of segments within the database.

## 9.2    RESTORE TECHNIQUES

With backup files and log archive partitions sorted on database page identifiers, single-pass restore merges database pages and log records in one pass over the entire device. With indexes on backup file and log archive, restore operations can recover database pages or segments in any order, with efficient access to all required backup images and log records. In other words, on-demand incremental restore operations execute the logic of single-pass restore one segment at a time, for segments required by query and transaction processing, with fast access to relevant backup and log archive information using the indexes on those files.

With segments restored in an unpredictable order, a mechanism is required to track which segments still require restore logic and which ones are fully recovered. A bitmap with a Boolean entry per segment is all that is required. This "segment recovery bitmap" is not persisted in the database yet its updates write new log records. For the case of a system failure during recovery from a media failure, checkpoints log the current state of the segment recovery bitmap, if need be in multiple pieces in order to fit it into log pages and log records.

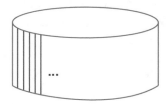

Figure 9.2: Segment recovery bitmap.

Figure 9.2 illustrates a storage device logically divided into many segments, with each segment comprising a number of individual database pages. In single-pass restore operations, a replacement device and its contents may become available to active transactions one segment at a time in strictly sequential order; in pure on-demand instant restore, segments (each with all the database pages it contains) become available one segment at a time in the order in which queries and transactions require and request database pages.

With multiple active user transactions, multiple restore operations may be active at the same time. In fact, it may occur that two user transactions attempt to restore the same segment at the same time. Thus, some concurrency control is required for the segment recovery bitmap. In fact, rather than introduce bit-level locking, it seems more practical to permit three states in the map: unrecovered, in recovery, and recovered. With three states, the granularity of locking in the map data structure seems simple. On the other hand, waking up threads waiting for recovery of a required segment suggests an implementation using the lock manager, i.e., a lock for each segment currently in recovery and only two states in the map.

## 9.3    RESTORE SCHEDULES

Pure on-demand restore operations permit query and transaction processing with the replacement device very quickly, but completion of the restore operation can take a long time. This is quite similar to pure on-demand restart operation after a system failure (see Section 5.2). Thus, quite similar to the combined, concurrent eager and lazy restart recovery, the recommended restore operation combines lazy, on-demand restore operations for segments required by users and applications with eager, bulk restore operation as in single-pass restore.

Figure 9.3 compares traditional recovery (see also Figure 2.5) with a combination of eager single-pass restore and concurrent on-demand, usage-guided restore. The transition from transaction processing to media recovery, including provisioning of replacement media, requires a short initial period. Thereafter, single-pass restore starts running in the background. Even running at low priority, single-pass recovery ought to be faster than traditional recovery with its multiple phases. Concurrently, as active transactions and queries attempt accesses to database pages not yet recovered, on-demand single-page repair provides data ahead of the background recovery process, not quite one page but one segment at a time.

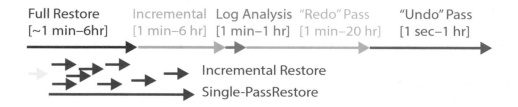

Figure 9.3: Concurrent eager and lazy restore.

Obviously, each segment requires only one restore operation. Thus, not only on-demand restore operations but also bulk restore operations must update the segment recovery bitmap. Moreover, bulk restore must participate in concurrency control in case multiple threads attempt to restore the same segment at the same time.

Since the bulk restore can proceed in any order, segment by segment, it is not required that the bulk restore logic proceed in the order of page identifiers as single-pass restore does. Instead, the bulk restore logic may focus on metadata (free space management, database catalogs), likelihood of use (e.g., b-tree root pages first), or specific databases, tables, indexes, or partitions. Moreover, the bulk restore logic may pause (and resume later without loss of work) or it may run in multiple threads, with policies depending on the hardware and the system load. In our prototype, a background thread restores one segment at a time as needed for active transactions; lacking any immediate need, it restores segments following the one most recently needed. For any policy, if the chosen segments are of sufficient size, bulk restore should require the same effort as single-pass restore.

## 9.4    SUMMARY OF INSTANT RESTORE

In summary, the required data structures for backup and log archive are similar to those for single-pass restore, except that these data structures need to be not just sorted but also indexed. For the backup, the suitable index is a b-tree. For the log archive, the suitable index is a partitioned b-tree. Creation of those indexes is practically free during backup and log archiving into a partially sorted log archive. For further efficiency, the log archive may also have a bit vector filter.

With those indexes, on-demand recovery restores one segment at a time, i.e., a pre-defined set of contiguous database pages. Within each segment, the restore algorithm is that of single-pass restore. The indexes enable efficient access to the relevant database pages in the backup and log records in the partitions of the log archive.

Moreover, since data structures and algorithms are so similar, segment-at-a-time restore operations can run both lazily, i.e., on demand and guided by active transactions, and eagerly, i.e., sweeping through all segments in the manner of single-pass restore. Thus, a restore operation should complete in about the same time as with offline single-pass restore, i.e., much faster than traditional restore operations with log replay and many random I/O operations, and on-demand restore guided by active transactions should not extend media recovery time.

Table 9.1: ARIES restore and instant restore

| | ARIES Restore | Instant Restore |
|---|---|---|
| Transaction logging | Same techniques and costs | |
| Database backups | Offline or online full, differential, or incremental backups | Offline or online full backups, indexed by database page identifier |
| Log archiving | Copy and compress original recovery log | Partial sort + aggregation + indexing of log records |
| Restoring backups | One backup at a time; merge possible | Merge short runs from backup and runs of the log archive |
| Log replay | In order of original execution—much random page I/O in the database | Merge short runs from backup and runs of the log archive |
| Active transactions | Suspended during restore, rollback after restore is complete | Online throughout, guiding restore operations |
| New transactions | Only after restore is complete | Online throughout, guiding restore operations |

Table 9.1, similar to Table 7.1, compares traditional ARIES media restore and instant restore. The first difference to Table 7.1 is that instant restore requires indexes on backups and the log archive. The second difference is that the merge logic combining backups and log archive runs for individual segments (short runs of database pages) rather than for once for all database pages on the replacement media. The third and crucial difference is that both active transactions affected by the failure and new transactions attempting to query or update the failed device may run and in fact guide the restore logic.

CHAPTER 10

# Applications of Instant Restore

The techniques of instant restore enable a few additional applications beyond media recovery.

## 10.1 PIPELINE EXTENSIONS

Single-pass restore runs as a continuous offline pipeline and thus permits the techniques of Section 8.1. These techniques appear at first sight incompatible with the online behavior of instant restore. Recovery proceeds segment-by-segment, in random sequence as guided by active transactions and in sequential sequence once recovery of the application's working set is complete. Thus, if restore operations append recovered segments to a new full backup, they do so in an unpredictable sequence. More importantly, new update transactions keep the target moving.

Indeed, an in-pipeline consistency check during instant restore is as difficult as any other online consistency check based on a disk-order database scan. For online consistency checking, checking data structures seems more appropriate, e.g., during each root-to-leaf traversal in a b-tree index.

On the other hand, instant restore can easily create a new full database backup. If the restore logical appends recovered segments to the backup in the order of their recovery, they will appear in apparently random sequent. However, since instant restore employs an index on the backup file, with an index entry for each segment, it seems straightforward to insert the required index entries. While single-pass restore inserts index entries in an ordered and thus most efficient manner, instant restore inserts index entries in random sequence. With 100–1,000,000 segments per media and thus 100–1,000,000 index entries, it seems that memory can hold the entire index and thus random insertions do not impose a substantial performance penalty.

More importantly, the result will be an online backup with incomplete transactions. Thus, should a subsequent restore operation rely on this backup, it needs to apply all "redo" log records written between start and completion of the backup operation. This applies, of course, to any restore operation starting from a backup taken online, i.e., with concurrent database updates.

## 10.2 HOT RESTORE

Traditional media recovery takes a long time with no progress possible for affected transactions. With instant restore, if replacement media are available immediately, active transactions may continue rather than abort. After all, a media failure need not terminate the database server, which can retain communication links and sessions as well as all server state in transaction manager, lock manager, buffer pool, etc. Thus, such transactions may resume as soon as the information required for on-demand restore is available in the log archive.

As a side note, hot restart (after a system failure or crash) is more difficult to realize. Resuming incomplete transactions (with serializable transaction isolation) requires re-acquisition of read-only locks, which are not visible in the recovery log but required for correct transaction isolation of continuing transactions. Even more difficult is re-establishing lost communication connections and login sessions without creation of vulnerabilities that a malicious intent can exploit.

## 10.3    RESTORE WITHOUT REPLACEMENT MEDIA

If no replacement media are available immediately, instant restore and write elision (see Section 4.2) together permit immediate query and transaction processing, at the expense of repeated recovery of the same database pages or segments. Upon a buffer fault, the buffer pool loads an out-of-date page image from the backup and brings up up-to-date using the log archive, just as in all forms of instant restore. Queries and transactions may read and modify the page image in the buffer pool using standard concurrency control and write-ahead logging. Upon the need for page eviction, the buffer pool replaces the dirty page without writing it.

Upon another buffer fault for the same database page, the process repeats, including the recovery actions already applied before. Due to this redundant work, this situation is undesirable, but continued query and transaction processing may be more important and valuable than some repetitive work. On the other hand, if buffer pool evictions are very rare because the buffer pool can hold the entire working set of the application, repeated recovery action should be rare.

## 10.4    ONLINE DATABASE MIGRATION

When migrating all data from one media (disk, table space, etc.) to another, there used to be three methods. The first method takes those data offline (no updates) for the duration of a copy operation, i.e., waits until active transaction end and prevents new transactions to access the data to be moved. The second method moves stale data at full copy speed and eventually catches up based on the recovery log. The third method temporarily applies each update in both places, at least for the data already copied.

Instant restore offers a new method, treating the source data as a backup and the destination space as replacement media. In other words, it "restores" into the new space with the old data serving the role of the backup. Of course, the recovery logic can combine guidance by active transactions and full bandwidth copying in the background, i.e., incremental on-demand restore logic and single-pass restore logic.

In fact, this method does not employ the full logic and capabilities of instant restore. For example, there is no need for an index on the backup since there is no compression. More significantly, there is no need for replaying log records from the log archive. Put differently, active transactions can continue (as in hot restore—Section 10.2). For segments not yet migrated, they read from the old media and write to the new media. Importantly, as in instant restore, online database migration marks clean pages in the buffer pool as dirty to forces them to the destination media.

If a partially complete migration aborts and needs to roll back, the same logic can migrate the data from the original destination back to the original source. The migration back to the original source uses as backup the segments already migrated to the original destination or the out-of-date contents of the original source. Inverting the segment recovery map of the original migration creates the initial segment recovery map for the migration back.

This new method avoids duplicate efforts for immediate maintenance of two copies or for log-based catch-up; yet it runs online guided by actual data usage as well as at full bandwidth while the system is otherwise idle.

## 10.5    SUMMARY OF INSTANT RESTORE APPLICATIONS

In summary, instant restore requires some minor changes from single-pass restore for immediate, up-to-date backups, but it also enables new solutions not possible with traditional restore or with single-pass restore. Transactions that access failed media actually may continue without much interruption; and online migration of databases, tables, and indexes may employ recovery techniques.

# CHAPTER 11

# Multiple Page, System, and Media Failures

Earlier chapters consider one failure at a time: a single-page failure (Chapter 3), a system failure (Chapter 5), or a media failure (Chapters 7 and 9). The present chapter considers failure and response during recovery from an earlier failure. It does not rise to a comprehensive analysis of multiple failures, i.e., any failure at any time during recovery from any earlier scenario with multiple failures. The first such analysis has yet to be written for any database recovery technique or set of techniques.

Among the four failure classes, i.e., transaction, system, media, and single-page failures, this discussion ignores transaction failures, since single-transaction rollback is present in all scenarios and readily feasible guided by the per-transaction chain of log records. In all cases, transaction rollback writes log records as it updates the database back to its original contents and then commits.

## 11.1 SINGLE-PAGE FAILURE DURING RESTORE

Recovery from a single-page failure on a device without a prior media failure can ignore any concurrent media failure and media recovery. A single-page failure within a segment not yet recovered seems impossible since recovery of the appropriate segment must precede any further logic verifying and accessing a database page. If a single-page failure is found after the surrounding segment has already been restored, then single-page recovery must run again, albeit for a single page rather than all pages in a segment. Note that single-page recovery already is a principal mechanism in instant restore.

The difference to single-page recovery as discussed in Chapter 3 is the presence of log archiving and of recycling space on the logging device. While the recovery log guides single-page recovery with per-transaction chains of log records, the log archive and its index format enable efficient search for log records pertaining to a specific database page. Thus, single-page recovery combines elements of single-pass restore, i.e., searching the log archive, and of the initial design of single-page recovery, i.e., traversing per-page chains of log records in the recovery log.

## 11.2 SINGLE-PAGE FAILURE DURING RESTART

A database page may fail a consistency check during restart, e.g., after a write operation remained incomplete due to a power failure that also led to system failure and restart. In that case, recovery starts the standard single-page recovery with an earlier page image, e.g., from a backup. If log archiving enables recycling space on the logging device, single-page recovery needs to employ the log archive as discussed earlier. Thus, a single-page failure during restart presents no problem.

## 11.3    MULTIPLE SYSTEM FAILURES

Recovery from a crash during restart requires no additional code—both traditional restart and instant restart handle earlier partial and failed restarts. Since log analysis does not modify any persistent data structures, it is quite possible that another restart attempt and its log analysis will similarly fail. The cause must be external, e.g., a power failure, or internal to the database management system, i.e., in formatting, writing, reading, or analyzing log records. External causes require changes outside the database management system; internal errors require repair of code defects.

A crash during "redo" or "undo" may need to consider log records preceding both the original crash and any subsequent crashes. The starting point for log analysis is always the last complete checkpoint, ignoring any subsequent incomplete checkpoint. A checkpoint immediately after log analysis avoids repeated log analysis of the same log records after a further system failure, i.e., while processing "redo," "undo," and new transactions.

If a system failure occurs after log analysis, the subsequent recovery and its log analysis will re-create the list of in-doubt pages and the list of incomplete transactions with their locks. These lists may differ from those during earlier recovery attempts due to completed single-page recovery (including writing recovered pages back to the database), completed transaction rollback (including new log records and possibly writing the affected database pages), and database changes by new transactions concurrent with the earlier recovery attempt. Based on log records written during transaction rollback and by new transactions, log analysis will correctly identify those pages and those transactions, and thus it will set up on-demand single-page "redo" recovery and on-demand single-transaction "undo" recovery precisely as required.

Frequent checkpoints during "redo" and "undo" might be a good policy. Similarly, during "redo" and "undo," the buffer pool might write dirty pages more actively than during normal transaction processing. Such policies may apply to recovery from any failure but particularly after multiple system failures.

If log analysis includes lock re-acquisition, i.e., if log analysis recovers all server state present in checkpoint log records, then the first post-crash checkpoint may follow immediately after log analysis. Log analysis after a second system failure can exploit such a checkpoint. Thus, log analysis after the second system failure scans only log records written by "undo" actions of the first restart and of new transactions after the first restart. In contrast, traditional (ARIES) restart entirely omits lock re-acquisition or (when optimized for new transactions during the "undo" phase) includes it in the "redo" phase. Thus, traditional restart cannot log new checkpoints until after the "redo" phase or even until after the "undo" phase.

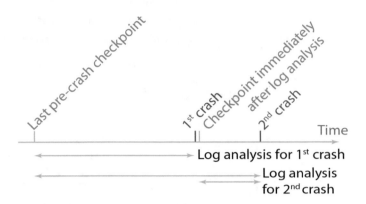

Figure 11.1: Log analysis in a second system failure.

Figure 11.1 illustrates how a second system failure takes advantage of the log analysis completed during a first system failure. The two bottom-most lines indicate the log analysis effort required after a 2nd system failure: the longer line indicates the effort without a checkpoint immediately after the 1st crash and its log analysis; the short line indicates the required effort if a new checkpoint was possible and completed immediately after the 1st crash and its log analysis. Even if multiple system failures occur, if each takes a database checkpoint immediately after log analysis, then each log record is scanned only once for log analysis.

## 11.4    MULTIPLE MEDIA FAILURES

A media failure during recovery from an earlier media failure similarly is covered by the restore functionality discussed so far. If one device fails while a restore operation writes to another device, the two device failures are independent and two independent instances of restore algorithms can recover from them.

If a replacement device fails while still the destination of a restore operation, the current restore operation may stop immediately and a new one can start with a new replacement device. This restore operation requires a new segment recovery bitmap. In other words, a segment recovery bitmap pertains to specific replacement media, and new replacement media (after a new media failure) imply a new segment recovery bitmap.

Incidentally, single-pass restore could produce a new, up-to-date database backup on the side. Database pages would appear in this backup in the same order as in the database, the old backup, and the partitions of the log archive. Instant restore could also produce a new backup as side effect, but this new database backup would contain segments in the order of recovery, i.e., in apparently random order. Nonetheless, it is still possible to produce an index for subsequent instant restore, i.e., segment by segment restore operation on demand by applications or transactions. Note that with a moderate number of segments (e.g., 1 M), the entire index fits in memory during backup and index creation.

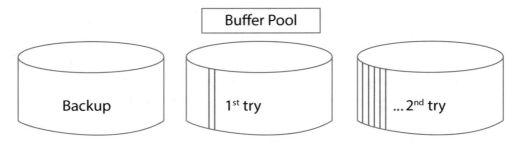

Figure 11.2: Multiple media failures.

Figure 11.2 illustrates a 2nd media failure after a 1st media recovery is partially complete. The 2nd recovery abandons both the initial replacement device and the segment recovery map built up during media recovery to that device. Another media recovery requires another replacement device and a new segment recovery map.

## 11.5   SYSTEM FAILURE DURING MEDIA RESTORE

As restoring the contents of a large database device may take hours, a system failure with a partially recovered replacement device is always possible. Fortunately, both single-pass restore and instant restore can resume without loss of work.

Specifically, even if the segment recovery bitmap is not permanent and thus maintained only in volatile memory, it is part of each checkpoint. Moreover, segment restoration is logged. Thus, log analysis can bring the in-memory segment recovery bitmap up-to-date. If a restore operation retains dirty database pages in the buffer pool and those are lost in the system failure, single-page recovery can restore them from backup and log archive.

As mentioned earlier, system restart must resume log archiving, i.e., restart the log archiving logic with the correct log records. This is entirely independent of any active restore operation and its continuation after a system restart.

## 11.6    MEDIA FAILURE DURING SYSTEM RESTART

Failure of database storage media during log analysis has no effect as log analysis only reads the recovery log. The appropriate techniques for media failure during traditional "redo" and "undo" (based on log scans) depend on immediate availability of replacement media.

If replacement media (as well as database backup and log archive) are immediately available, the restart logic can access database pages only within segments already recovered by the restore logic, i.e., merging appropriate parts of the database backup and of partitions of the log archive. Once the restore logic has a segment up-to-date with the end of the log archive, the restart logic may apply remaining "redo" actions and, for transactions failed with the system failure, "undo" actions.

If replacement media are not available, "redo" and "undo" actions for pages on the failed device must wait. All "redo" actions must wait until replacement media become available. Active transactions might be able to finish without further activity requiring the failed media; otherwise, active transactions can wait for that time or they can roll back immediately.

Alternatively, as mentioned in Section 4.4, when a non-essential volume is not available during restart recovery, transaction-by-transaction "undo" can defer "undo" actions. In addition to attaching deferred "undo" actions to branch nodes in a b-tree, to be pushed down when their child nodes are accessed, restart with missing volumes requires attaching deferred "undo" actions to volumes. An implementation might use a catalog of volumes or some other mechanism to identify volumes and invoke the deferred "redo" and "undo" actions when volumes are mounted.

## 11.7    SUMMARY OF RECOVERY AFTER MULTIPLE FAILURES

In summary, repeated system failures or repeated media failures simply require re-starting the standard restart or restore algorithms. A repeated restart may benefit from a checkpoint taken immediately after log analysis in the first restart attempt. A repeated restore operation requires new replacement media and a new segment recovery bitmap.

A combination of media and system failure requires that each page access first invokes the restore logic combining database backup and log archive and then the restart logic using single-page recovery based on the recent pre-crash recovery log. The segment recovery bitmap prevents redundant invocations of the restore logic (just as in every other case of instant restore) and PageLSN values prevent redundant invocations of the restart logic (just as in every other case of instant restart).

# CHAPTER 12

# Instant Failover

Instant failover assumes a pair of nodes and log shipping similar to Figure 8.3: using a buffer pool, the database, and a recovery log, a primary node executes queries and updates while one or more secondary nodes hold a database backup and the log archive. Their principal communication is continuous log shipping from the primary to the secondary nodes. The principal performance metric is how quickly a secondary node can take over query and transaction processing after discovery that the primary node or its communication has failed.

In the traditional approach to high availability and fast failover, each secondary node holds a complete copy of the database and always keeps it up-to-date by immediate application of all log records received via log shipping. An alternative is mirroring—instead of log records, the primary node ships database pages as it writes them to its local database. Compared to log shipping, mirroring saves the effort on each secondary node, i.e., reading database pages that require changes and then applying received log records. On the other hand, mirroring ships entire pages even when only a few bytes have changed. Moreover, both mirroring and log shipping require a full up-to-date copy of the database on each secondary node.

In some fortuitous cases, these additional database copies can serve query processing and thus offload the primary server. Note that concurrency control conflicts between such queries and updates received from the primary server must terminate the queries. Thus, splitting a workload in this way works best with snapshot isolation and multi-version concurrency control. Moreover, without such a workload of read-only transactions, the secondary servers maintain their up-to-date database copies purely for the chance of a possible failover.

In the new design, instant failover, a secondary node does not require an up-to-date copy of the database. It merely requires empty space for a new copy of the database, a full database backup (days, weeks, or even months old), and a log archive covering the entire interval since the full database backup. Both database backup and log archive must support fast access by page identifier, typically using indexes similar to those required for instant restore.

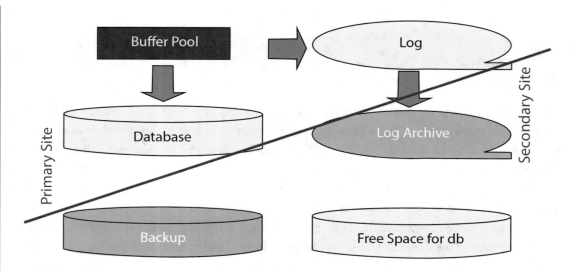

Figure 12.1: Nodes and data for instant failover.

Figure 12.1 illustrates an example system setup that enables instant failover, with the diagonal red line separating primary and secondary sites. The primary node runs application transactions using its buffer pool, the database, and the recovery log. Each secondary node holds a backup and continuously builds up its copy of the log archive. The free space remains untouched until a failover actually occurs. It might be useful to compare this diagram to Figure 2.6—the differences are the sorted and indexed log archive and the free space instead of an up-to-date copy of the database.

Failover requires recovery of both server state and database contents. The server state includes transaction manager, lock manager, and buffer pool. Recovery or re-initialization of server state is quite similar to system restart. Recovery of database contents is quite similar to media restore operations. Thus, instant failover must combine log information and recovery actions from both instant restart and instant restore, with some additional concerns and considerations.

By default, failover to a secondary node must terminate and roll back incomplete transactions. Thus, log shipping must include database checkpoints as well as all required transaction information. In particular, log shipping must also include "undo" information until a transaction is complete, i.e., its commit log record acknowledged by the secondary node. On the other hand, if failover is very fast, transactions might continue on the secondary node after the failover. In general, such a "hot failover" requires failover of communication and sessions, in addition to failover of transactions, database, and recovery log. A promising intermediate solution continues only selected transactions, e.g., those that do not modify logical database contents but modify the database representation, e.g., index creation or removal.

## 12.1    LOG SHIPPING AND LOG ARCHIVING

The foundation of up-to-date failover is log shipping. The primary node executes transactions, logs and commits their database changes in the local recovery log, maintains the database, and sends the log records to the secondary node. The secondary node receives the log records and archives them in a log archive as described for instant restore, i.e., partially sorted and indexed by a partitioned b-tree.

The log records sent from primary node to secondary node must include checkpoint information, i.e., incomplete transactions and their non-read-only locks. Checkpoint information about in-doubt pages is not required because media recovery re-creates database contents from a backup and the log archive, not from the database and its recovery log. Similarly, the primary node need not send log records about pages written back to the database.

The log records sent from primary node to secondary node must include transaction commit log record and, for log records of uncommitted transactions, transaction identifiers and "undo" information. The actual log archiving process may reduce the log records. In principle, a secondary node may apply all log compression described for instant restore. For example, once it has received the commit log record for a particular transaction, there is no need to retain "undo" information. If, however, the secondary node writes "redo" information to its persistent log archive before it receives the commit log record, it must include "undo" information and the recovery logic during failover becomes more complex.

Even after writing log records to the log archive, a secondary node retains the recovery log as received for the current checkpoint interval. In other words, when it receives a complete checkpoint, it may discard log records written to the log archive and preceding the checkpoint in the original recovery log. Depending on the memory available in the secondary node, the log volume, and the checkpoint interval, an implementation may turn the log records of each checkpoint interval into a run within the log archive and a partition in the partitioned b-tree indexing the log archive.

## 12.2    RECOVERY OF SERVER STATE IN A FAILOVER

The relevant server state for restart and failover covers the transaction manager, the lock manager, and the buffer pool—in other words, the set of active transactions other than read-only transactions, the set of locks held by active transactions (except read-only locks), and the set of in-doubt database pages (remaining dirty in the database buffer pool). Instant failover recovers server state using techniques adapted from instant restart.

In instant restart (Chapter 5), log analysis recovers the required server state such that transaction processing can resume immediately with concurrent "redo" recovery actions (in the form of single-page repair) and "undo" actions (in the form of single-transaction rollback). ARIES and its variants and implementations recover only the transaction manager during log analysis. The "redo" scan over the recovery log identifies in-doubt pages and checks them immediately. The lock manager does not need recovery if new transactions must wait until all recovery phases are complete. For new transactions already during the "undo" phase, ARIES permits lock re-acquisition during the "redo" phase [MHL 92].

For instant failover, the new primary (formerly secondary) node may perform log analysis either continuously while receiving log records, i.e., before the failover, or as part of taking over primary responsibility for the database, i.e., after the failover decision. Mixed models are possible. For example, a secondary node may track the set of active transactions continuously during log shipping yet acquire locks only after a failover. With such a design, a secondary node avoids expensive lock management yet can acquire locks for active transactions quickly based on log records of active transactions. These log records are readily available using the per-transaction log chains. Lock acquisition after a failover does not necessarily require checkpoint log records in the log-shipping stream or a complete scan of all log records since the most recent database checkpoint, but the checkpoint log records can help.

Long-running transactions may require special techniques for efficient failover. Instead of tracing the per-transaction log chain backward to log records minutes or even hours old, it seems more efficient to exploit checkpoint log records that list the set of non-read-only locks for each active transaction. These checkpoint log records may be the standard database checkpoints or they may be special per-transaction checkpoints, applied only to long-running transactions and containing the same information as the log records for database checkpoint. A per-transaction checkpoint log record should be part of the per-transaction chain of log records. Per-transaction log analysis ends when encountering such a per-transaction checkpoint. Thus, a long-running transaction should write a per-transaction checkpoint about as frequently as the system takes database checkpoints. It may be possible to simplify and speed up database checkpoints even in single-node deployments using such per-transaction checkpoints.

Tracking in-doubt pages modified by recent and active transactions is not required during instant failover. Instead, instant failover includes instant restore and all database pages require recovery.

## 12.3    RECOVERY OF DATABASE CONTENTS IN A FAILOVER

Transaction processing after a failover assumes that the database on the new primary node is up-to-date and transaction-consistent. Instant failover starts with a full database backup and a log archive, with some log records still being sorted in order to form a partially sorted log archive indexed by a partitioned b-tree. Those log records may still linger in memory, i.e., the failover node has received them but has not added them to the persistent log archive yet. Instant failover recovers database contents using techniques adapted from instant restore.

The first task toward database recovery during instant failover sorts and indexes those log records. They may remain in memory and not immediately be added to the persistent log archive.

The important aspect is that the restore logic can readily access all log records received from the failed former primary node.

The second task provisions database media for future database storage, recovery log, and log archiving. If additional nodes require further log shipping, the new primary node sets up appropriate connections and log shipping streams.

The third task initiates single-pass restore in the background. It will run until all restore operations are complete. It will coordinate with on-demand incremental restore operations by avoiding concurrent recovery of the same database segment, by marking database segments it recovered, and by skipping over database segments already recovered by on-demand incremental restore operations.

The logic of single-pass restore during instant failover is the same as during media recovery (Chapter 7). Thus, it reads the database backup in large units of I/O, merges partitions of the log archive with one another and with the backup pages, and writes the replacement database in similarly large units of I/O, i.e., with high bandwidth.

The fourth task of instant failover resumes transaction processing. When a transaction invokes the buffer pool for a database page not yet recovered, the logic of instant restore recovers the appropriate database segment on demand, exploiting appropriate indexes on the backup and on the partitions of the log archive. When a transaction requests a lock conflicting with one of the transactions active prior to the failover, that transaction must rollback. Transaction rollback may invoke restore operations for one or multiple segments by invoking the buffer pool for database pages not yet recovered.

The final task of instant failover rolls back pre-failover transactions not yet aborted on demand upon lock conflicts with new transactions. If desired, this task may start earlier, in which case it may well trigger restore operations for individual database segments. On the other hand, earlier execution of this task focuses early recovery efforts on the application's working set within the database. Of course, all pre-failover transactions must write rollback log records just as during rollback without failover.

## 12.4    SUMMARY OF INSTANT FAILOVER

In summary, instant failover requires log shipping before the failure and techniques from instant restart and instant restore after the failover. As in traditional log shipping, a transaction is durable even in the event of a complete node failure only after the secondary node has received all its log records including the commit log record. As in instant restart, log analysis recovers server state, in particular the transaction manager's set of active transactions and these transactions' non-read-only locks. As in instant restore, a partially sorted and indexed log archive permits log replay by merging backup and partitions of the log archive, both as required by active transactions and in bulk in the background.

Log analysis can rely on continuous inspection of the stream of log records or on post-failover analysis of log records between the most recent checkpoint and the end of the log-shipping stream, which assumes that log shipping transmits checkpoint log records. In the recommended hybrid technique, each secondary node continuously tracks active transactions with acquisition of locks only after a failover indeed occurred. This hybrid avoids the need for checkpoint log records in the log-shipping stream as well as the overhead of continuous acquisition and release of locks in the secondary node.

Log shipping for instant failover using these techniques requires much fewer resources on the secondary node than traditional log shipping. Instant failover merely requires a database backup, whereas traditional log shipping and failover requires an active database; and instant failover merely merges backup and log archive partitions in quasi-sequential I/O operations, whereas log replay in traditional log shipping and in traditional failover requires either many random I/O operations or an extremely large, dedicated buffer pool. Nonetheless, failover latency is quite similar in both techniques, gated by the delay in log shipping, and transaction processing performance after the failover suffers only slightly immediately after instant restart.

Table 12.1: Comparison of failover techniques

|  | Traditional Mirroring | Traditional Log Shipping | Instant Failover |
| --- | --- | --- | --- |
| Load on primary node before failure | Send entire pages | Send log records | |
| Load on secondary node before failure | Write received pages (random I/O) | Page updates: read, redo, write | Log archiving: sort + aggregate + index |
| Load after failover | Ship pages to create an additional mirror | Ship database backup and newer log records | Ship new log records |
| Vulnerability | Until an additional database copy exists and becomes up-to-date | | Only during failover itself |
| Cost (plus backups, log, log archive) | Multiple up-to-date database copies | | One up-to-date database copy |
| Per-node hardware requirements | Substantial CPU and I/O on each secondary node | | Little CPU and I/O on secondary nodes |
| Network hardware requirements | Page copies, new backup | Log shipping, new backup | Log shipping |

Table 12.1 compares three alternative approaches for high availability. Traditional mirroring sends entire page images to all secondary nodes whenever the primary node writes dirty pages from its buffer pool to its local storage. In contrast, log shipping sends only the actual changes, encoded in log records. Traditional log shipping simply applies and saves the received log records, whereas each secondary node preparing for instant failover sorts and indexes the log records, possibly after aggregating them, e.g., suppressing a "do" and a matching "undo" log records. Importantly, if there is no up-to-date database on the secondary node, there is no need or opportunity to apply the received log records or to read and write database pages.

The most significant differences are the vulnerability immediately after failover and the overall system cost. With the traditional techniques, the system is "down one copy" after a failover until creation of a new up-to-date copy of the database completes. Thus, the system is more vulnerable to data loss immediately after a failover just when a failure is most likely due to the correlation among failures observed in practice. In contrast, instant failover creates the new database copy incrementally yet with immediate availability for queries and transaction processing at the new primary node. Thus, there is no additional vulnerability during failover and recovery.

This difference has implications for the overall system cost. While the traditional techniques require multiple copies, e.g., 3 or 5 copies in order to prevent data loss in multiple failures, instant failover requires only a single up-to-date database plus database backups and log archives accessible to multiple possible failover destinations. Moreover, less data processed and maintained in each secondary node reduces the hardware requirements in each node as well as the network bandwidth required before or after a failover.

# CHAPTER 13

# Applications of Instant Failover

In principle, log shipping and instant failover apply to all networks, including wide-area networks and distributed data centers. The following focuses on failures and failover in scalable clusters of co-located nodes, each with local storage and processing power.

For the mechanisms that Chapter 12 introduces, there are many possible policies. For example, if an application needs both high availability and scalable capacity, some secondary nodes may provide only high availability by instant failover while some other secondary nodes may also provide high query capacity by maintaining an up-to-date database and processing queries on it. The present chapter introduces additional mechanisms and again leaves policies to applications, deployment models, and database administrators.

## 13.1 INSTANT FAILBACK

After a failover, the original primary node may recover (reboot, reconnect) faster than the new primary node can restore even half of the database. In such a case, the original primary node may resume its assigned workload and finish all recovery faster than the original secondary node. The required mechanism is another failover back to the original primary node. Local storage contents at the original node may initially be out-of-date and the original node needs to catch up.

A traditional implementation technique first applies updates processed during failure and reboot, and then applies updates processed during the first catch-up phase, etc., until the required catch-up set is small and stopping the workload for a sufficient period is acceptable. Instead, catch-up can be incremental and run on demand, with a background thread catching up those database pages not immediately required by query and transaction processing.

Importantly, if the original database remains mostly intact, e.g., after a system failure (software crash), or if even the buffer pool remains warm, e.g., after a failover due to a network failure, the failback operation and its recovery logic may not even touch much of the database on persistent storage. Only the log records created between failover and failback need "redo" recovery. If the working set of an application fits in memory, most of the failback logic can execute in memory without access to persistent storage.

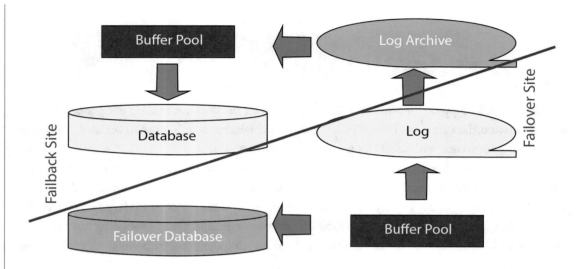

Figure 13.1: Recovery of data in a restarted (formerly failed) node.

Figure 13.1 illustrates this situation. The original primary node (top left) still has its database and perhaps even its buffer pool. The original secondary node (bottom right) has recovered much of the application's working set in its buffer pool as well as a few segments on persistent storage. Failback can exploit the up-to-date segments and database pages in the original (and final) primary node and needs to apply only the log records created on the failover node.

Thus, the original primary node needs to act as secondary node from failover to failback, i.e., while the original secondary node processes transaction and generates new log records. If a network disruption caused the failover, the original primary node needs to catch up such that it holds all log records required for correct media recovery.

If the original primary node fails again soon after a failback, the original failover node can resume its failover. Of course, the failover nodes requires all log records from the original primary node. Database segments restored during the first failover may be still up-to-date and thus do not require further recovery effort after the second failover. The required bookkeeping combines the segment recovery map with the log records created by the original primary node between the failback and the second failover. Note that failback to the original primary node is similar to aborting a database migration, i.e., migration back to the original media (Section 10.4).

## 13.2    FAILOVER POOLS

For the fastest possible failover, a secondary node may pre-start a database server process with no information yet in transaction manager, lock manager, and buffer pool—at least none of it for the database failing over. Such a server can take over for any database. A pre-started database server might serve other databases before and after it takes over for a failed database. Thus, instant failover may add information into the server state of an active server, which might require evicting some information from within this server, in particular database pages from the buffer pool.

In general, there might be not just a single secondary node but multiple nodes. In case of a failure of the primary node, one of the secondary nodes must take over. We ignore here the question on how to choose among multiple secondary nodes and focus on techniques and mechanisms for instant failover on the chosen secondary node.

Conversely, a single node may partition its data such that failover spreads responsibility widely to multiple secondary nodes. In this case, log shipping must split the log records to the correct secondary nodes. The remainder discusses failing over an entire database but it might be only a partition within a database.

Finally, a node may serve as a secondary node for multiple databases or even multiple primary nodes. This assumes, of course, that this node holds backups of all pertinent databases and receives a log-shipping stream from all relevant databases and nodes. If node failures are rare and independent of each other such that double failures are exceedingly rare, such a design promises to be viable.

Two possible deployment options suggest themselves. First, a large set of primary nodes serve the database workload with only a few secondary nodes. All secondary nodes have access to all backups and all log archives, e.g., in shared network-attached storage. If one of the primary nodes fails, any of the secondary nodes can take over and assume the role of the specific failed node. With this deployment design, a few extra servers may achieve high availability rather than twice or thrice the number of required servers as in traditional designs for high availability.

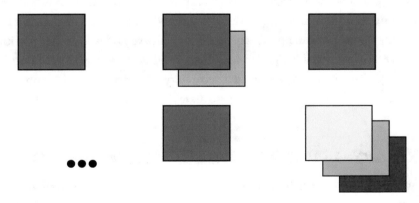

Figure 13.2: A small failover pool for many primary nodes.

Figure 13.2 illustrates a large set of working nodes (blue), each serving as primary node for its partition of the database, and a small set of stand-by nodes (yellow, green, and red), each ready to serve as failover node. Some of the working nodes might have up-to-date copies (using traditional log shipping or mirroring) that provide additional read-only capacity but can also server as failover nodes; one such node is shown (green) in the top row. All stand-by nodes require access to the backups and log archives of all working nodes. Thus, as in this example, each working node could archive its own recovery log into shared storage.

Second, a large set of nodes may serve as secondary nodes for one another, in such a way that each node has multiple partitions and any failure spreads the load across multiple nodes. Thus, even with a small number of failures, service continues with reasonable performance. Each partition requires multiple secondary nodes such that load balancing after is possible in cases of multiple node failures. Of course, until failover, a partition requires log archiving in a secondary node.

## 13.3   ELASTICITY

Failover, failback, multiple partitions per node, etc. are valuable not only for failures but also for elastic database deployments, i.e., load balancing in the absence of failures, while one database or partition experiences high temporary workloads. Note that some designs for elasticity distinguish "stateful" storage nodes and stateless processing nodes, elastically growing and shrinking the processing nodes but not the storage nodes. Instant failover and related techniques permit elastically growing and shrinking the set of storage nodes.

The essential idea, of course, is to divide the workload into more partitions than there are nodes in the cluster and to initiate failover of individual partitions from a heavily loaded node to a lightly loaded node. The latter may be a node only recently added in order to grow the cluster.

For shrinking a cluster, the approach is to remove all workloads from a node by failing its partitions over to other nodes. As a cluster shrinks and nodes exit, these nodes must shed responsibilities as primary nodes for some partitions and as secondary nodes for other partitions. Failing over the role of secondary node is simpler with instant failover than with traditional techniques for high availability. Giving a newly designated secondary node access to a backup and the log archive is easier than transferring a complete, up-to-date copy of the database and the maintenance responsibility for it.

## 13.4   SUMMARY OF INSTANT FAILOVER APPLICATIONS

In summary, while most instant failover techniques improve availability of databases and their applications, the techniques in this section also improve load balancing and data center costs.

# CHAPTER 14

# File Systems and Data Files

Many modern file systems rely on journaling for failure-atomic writes to multiple pages. Contrary to the occasional misunderstanding, journaling is not equal to write-ahead logging. In write-ahead logging, log records persist beyond a transaction and its commit logic, whereas file system journals erase all information once propagated into the file system. In other words, failure-atomic writes provide the "A" (atomicity) of transactions' "ACID" properties but fail to ensure or even contribute to the "D" (durability). Further differences are the well-defined transaction concept in databases, user-defined transaction boundaries, a fine granularity of locking, i.e., smaller than a page, e.g., record-level locking or key-value locking, and the ability to ensure continued absence (for phantom protection, serializability, and "repeatable count" transaction isolation) other than by inserting dummy files with the appropriate file names.

The following assumes a file system with write-ahead logging and a long-lived recovery log or a log archive. With log records that persist in the recovery log or a log archive, file systems can provide the benefits of single-page recovery, instant restart, instant restore, and instant failover not only to their internal structured information but also to their data blocks filled with user-defined or unstructured information.

Database-like information in a file system can use database techniques. This includes free space management as well as directories and other metadata, even indirection blocks within large data files. Beyond logging, this applies to many database concepts for both concurrency control and recovery. It also applies to indexing, including normalization, de-normalization (e.g., merged indexes or b-trees of multiple record types in a single sort order), compression (including prefix and suffix truncation specific to sorted indexes such as b-trees), update optimizations (e.g., partitioned b-trees similar to log-structured b-trees, but with all partitions within a single b-tree and with incremental merge steps as side effect of query execution), etc.

The remainder of this section focuses on data blocks with user-defined or unstructured contents but without page header and thus without space for PageLSN values, which are required for exactly-once application of updates and fundamental for all recovery techniques in earlier sections. The principal technique is to augment each pointer to a data block in order to enable both fault detection and repair.

## 14.1    FAULT DETECTION

Each file has a collection of pointers to data blocks. Often a single pointer and a counter of contiguous data blocks is called an extent. Fault detection and repair can focus on individual data blocks, on entire extents, or on fragments of a few data blocks.

The general approach is to adapt the techniques of self-repairing b-tree indexes (Section 4.1) into self-repairing data files. With data blocks filled to capacity with user contents and without space for a PageLSN value, a file system can embed a cyclic redundancy check (CRC) value with each child pointer. Alternative parity calculations are equally possible, with the obvious tradeoffs between size and assurance, i.e., the danger of undetected faults due to equal parity values. Note that a parity value is required for each fragment, i.e., each unit of fault detection and repair.

Like nodes in self-repairing b-tree indexes, self-repairing data files must employ only a single pointer to each extent or fragment. With that pointer, there must be a parity value for each fragment. Each access can readily verify whether a fragment's contents match the parity value.

The fragment size can be difficult design decision. On one hand, large fragments reduce the storage overhead for parity values. On the other hand, small fragments reduce the overhead of parity verification. Thus, it seems worthwhile to permit fragments of multiple pages as well as multiple fragments in an allocation extent.

## 14.2    FAULT REPAIR

If a data access detects that the current contents of the data page has an unexpected parity value, single-page recovery brings the data page up-to-date using the recovery log or log archive. Discussions below address contents and size of log records. The first difficulty is to find the most recent log record for a data page. One obvious option is to augment each pointer to a data page with an expected LSN value. This is similar to ChildLSN values in self-repairing indexes; any differences are due to the distinctions of data page, fragment, and extent.

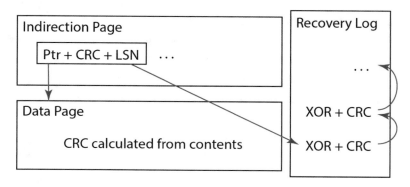

Figure 14.1: Augmented pointers to data pages.

Figure 14.1 illustrates a parent page, usually called an indirection block, within a self-repairing file. The data page contains only data and therefore no page header of any kind. The indirection block attaches to each pointer to a data page a CRC value and an LSN value. When fetching the data page in the buffer pool guided by the indirection block, the file system verifies that the stored page image satisfies the cyclic redundancy check. If not, it recovers the correct and up-to-date contents for the data page by traversing the chain of log records pertaining to the data page and, if the data page has been in use since before the last file system backup, by fetching an older page image from a file system backup.

## 14.3   LOGGING SMALL UPDATES

For a partial page update, the contents for the log records may be computed using an "exclusive or" operation of old and new page contents. Within an "x-or" image, run-length encoding can readily compress the unmodified parts of the data page. Both "redo" and "undo" can use such a log record; there is no separate "redo" and "undo" information. Moreover, recovery may apply multiple such log records in any sequence and log archiving can easily aggregate such log records.

In ARIES recovery, a PageLSN value is akin to a timestamp or a version number and permit guaranteed exactly-only application of each update. Without page header or PageLSN value, guarantees for exactly-once updates must rely on parity values. If an access finds a data page with a parity value other than the expected value, traversal of the page-by-page log chain goes to most recent backup or to a log record that matches the parity value on the page image. In other words, updates must include the post-update parity value in each log record. While not absolutely guaranteed, parity values of 64 or 128 bits provide sufficient certainty. If not, it is also possible to copy some bytes from each data page into its pointer page in order to create space for a PageLSN value on the data page.

## 14.4   LOGGING LARGE UPDATES

While file updates smaller than a page can be logged similarly to database updates, there clearly is a need and opportunity for optimizations for large file operations, in particular for newly allocated pages, e.g., in file creation. Overwriting a file may use copy-on-write, i.e., a transactional file system may write a separate copy and delete the original file when the overwriting transaction commits.

When writing a newly allocated data page, traditional logging writes two copies of the page to the recovery log (because the log is usually mirrored) and then another copy during log archiving (which usually uses a RAID-6 device). Thus, logging is more expensive than mirroring for new pages. A new technique, instant log archiving or direct log archiving, reverses this imbalance by writing the new page contents directly to the log archive, of course in runs sorted and indexed on page identifier. In addition, it writes a short log records to the recovery log about the page allocation and the archived page contents. Thus, new pages are written not four times (as required when logging and archiving in dual copy), not three times (as required for mirroring resilient to two failures, as used in many reliable file systems) but only two times (in the data store and the log archive) plus some redundancy required by RAID for the log archive, e.g., RAID-6. Instant log archiving holds an advantage over traditional mirroring file systems by its a reduction in overall write volume, in addition to the other benefits of instant recovery such as instant single-page repair, instant system restart, instant media restore, instant node failover, obsolete incremental backups, and remote virtual backups.

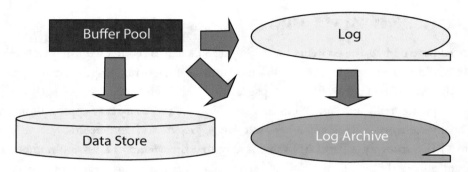

Figure 14.2: Direct log archiving for new data pages.

Figure 14.2 illustrates data movement in direct log archiving of new file pages. One copy of each page goes into the file system and one to the log archive. The latter implies some redundancy and additional write volume in the RAID device. A small log record in the recovery log links the transaction, the update, and the page image in the log archive.

Direct log archiving seems promising not only for new data pages in a file system but also in a database. For example, if performance tuning leads to a new secondary index for one of the database tables, the traditional optimization relies on allocation-only logging during the actual index creation and later copying the new index into the log archive. Thus, the traditional technique requires scanning the entire new index during log backup. The new technique writes the new index pages immediately to two locations, i.e., to the database and to the log archive.

## 14.5    SUMMARY OF INSTANT RECOVERY IN FILE SYSTEMS

In summary, instant recovery and all its individual techniques apply to not only databases but also file systems. Instead of file system journaling, which really just writes each page twice, instant recovery requires write-ahead logging with archiving all log records between backup operations. Structured data within a file system, e.g., directories and file properties can use tables and indexes.

Unstructured and user-defined file contents, stored in data pages without page headers and thus without PageLSN value, log small updates using XOR and large updates using direct archiving. Cyclic redundancy check or other parity values enable continuous incremental consistency checks.

CHAPTER   15

# Performance and Scalability

This chapter shows typical performance results for instant restart and instant restore, each with a large buffer pool holding the application's entire working set and with a small buffer pool that incurs buffer faults during transaction processing. The intention here is not a comprehensive evaluation of performance, scalability, or tradeoffs; the purpose here is to demonstrate that instant restart and instant restore, both based on single-page repair and single-transaction rollback, promise substantially shorter perceived downtimes than possible with traditional ARIES techniques. In other words, instant recovery improves system availability by improving the perceived mean time to repair. It is orthogonal to other techniques that might improve the mean time to failure.

The experimental hardware is a dual-socket Intel Xeon X5670 with 24 hardware threads and 96 GB of DRAM. Log and database are on 256-GB Samsung 840 Pro SSDs. The operating system is Ubuntu Linux 14.04 Kernel 3.13.0. The buffer pool is 70 GB and thus larger than the database; the log buffer is 20 GB and thus larger than the recovery log in the tests below. The test database is TPC-C scale factor 100 with 13 GB initial size and a growth rate of about 1,200 pages (9.6 MB) per second. The recovery log grows to 19 GB in 5 minutes or about 65 MB/s. Checkpoints are taken every 5 seconds; these checkpoints log lists of dirty database pages in the buffer pool rather than force those pages to storage. The buffer pool forces a dirty database page to storage only when evicting the page; there is no active page cleaner. Thus, "redo" after a restart must repeat 19 GB of log records, whereas "undo" is negligible due to a workload exclusively running short transactions.

## 15.1   SYSTEM FAILURE AND RESTART

The first experiment runs a transaction processing workload and forces a system failure after 5 minutes. The results are typical for all kinds of databases and eventually file systems—neither the best possible nor the worst possible.

Figure 15.1 illustrates transaction rates before, during, and after recovery from a system failure. During the first 5 minutes, the system runs normally, processing transactions, writing log records, taking system checkpoints, etc. Then a software crash occurs and restart begins immediately.

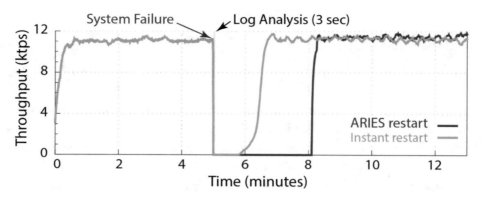

Figure 15.1: Transaction processing rates before and after restart.

ARIES shows more than 3 minutes before new transactions can run. The "undo" phase takes only the last 3 seconds of that time; therefore, ARIES variants that permit new transactions during the "undo" phase would make no practical difference in this case.

Instant restart spends a substantial time loading old log records. Log analysis loads only the log records back to the last good pre-crash checkpoint; "redo" requires many more and much older log records because the buffer pool logic in this experiment is very lazy cleaning dirty pages. Once all required log records are cached, "redo" recovery guided by new transactions kicks in and the transaction rate grows very quickly.

A larger buffer pool with more database pages, including more dirty database pages at the time of the software crash, would extend recovery times. A buffer pool with more aggressive page cleaning would reduce "redo" recovery in both restart technologies.

## 15.2   MEDIA FAILURE AND RESTORE

The second experiment runs that same transaction processing workload and forces a media failure after 10 minutes. Again, these results are typical for all kinds of databases and eventually file systems—neither the best possible nor the worst possible.

Figure 15.2 illustrates transaction rates before, during, and after recovery from a media failure. During the first 10 minutes, the system runs normally at about 12,000 transactions per second. Then a media failure occurs and the system immediately invokes recovery to a "cold stand-by" (formatted but empty) replacement disk.

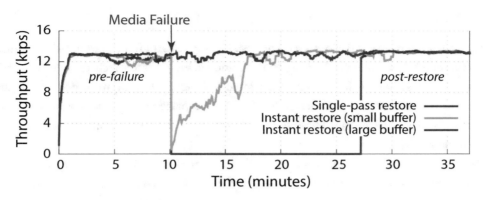

Figure 15.2: Transaction processing rates before and after restore.

The diagram does not show traditional restore, which would take hours. Even IBM's "fast log apply" would take perhaps an hour to completion, which would also be the time to the first new transaction querying or updating the data.

In contrast, single-pass recovery (red curve) takes about 17 minutes to complete media recovery including log replay. Hardware bandwidth on the backup device and the replacement device limit the performance of single-pass recovery. After recovery, the transaction rate returns to normal almost immediately.

Instant restore (green curve) enables new transactions immediately, including both read-only and read-write transactions, with quickly increasing transaction rates. Of course, instant restore also requires 17 minutes or a little more to complete the restore operation, but at least the application is up-and-running right away.

Instant restore with a large buffer pool (blue curve) shows how transaction processing may continue, practically without interruption, if the buffer pool can hold the entire working set of the application. Since page images resident in the buffer pool do not require any restore operation, the application may use them with triggering restore logic for individual pages or segments. In the background, single-pass restore recovers the lost media contents to a replacement device.

In a system with large storage devices, the differences would be even more dramatic. For example, a modern disk drive with large capacity and high transfer bandwidth requires 8 TB/250 MB/s = 32,000 sec ≈ 9 hours just to restore a backup, i.e., not counting log replay. In other words, a system with state-of-the-art large disk drives would be offline for at least 9 hours offline time versus immediate read-write transactions.

In a system with large memory and a large database buffer pool, the increase in transaction rates would come even faster. For example, if the working set fits in the buffer pool, the full transaction rate comes practically instantaneously.

## 15.3    SUMMARY OF PERFORMANCE AND SCALABILITY

In summary, instant recovery performs as expected. During restart after a system failure, transaction rates start to climb immediately after log analysis and caching old log records required for "redo." Recovery completes about as fast as with traditional techniques. During restore after a media failure, transaction rates start to climb immediately after a replacement device is available. Recovery completes much faster with single-pass restore than with traditional restore techniques including IBM's fast log apply.

Not surprisingly, during recovery from a failure, transaction rates do not equal those of failure-free systems. The value of instant recovery is the ability to conduct business rather than not run any queries or transactions at all. In other words, a business user will compare the transaction rates during recovery with a system that is offline as in traditional recovery rather than with a failure-free system.

# CHAPTER 16

# Conclusions

In summary, modern hardware triggered research into detection and recovery of single-page failures, which created opportunities for on-demand, incremental, seemingly instant recovery from system and media failures. Moreover, efficient single-page recovery creates opportunities for more reliable data stores, e.g., in the form of self-repairing indexes, and for more efficient operations, e.g., using write elision and read elision.

For incremental recovery from media failures, two further innovations were required: indexing backup files and partially sorted, indexed log archives. Partially sorted log archives, optionally indexed for on-demand use, permit both efficient creation from the active recovery log and efficient use during restore operations. Archiving employs principally the logic of run generation well known from external merge sort; restoration employs principally the merge logic well known from external merge sort and, in database query processing, merge join.

Efficient restore operations even from a very large log archive enables efficient log replay: instead of many random I/O operations in the database, database pages from the backup media and log records from the log archive only require merging. Large units of I/O ensure restore bandwidth near the limits of the devices employed. Thus, there is no longer any use for differential and incremental backup media; restore operation may simply merge the last full backup with the log archive. Similar logic also permits creating an up-to-date full backup without touching the active database; merging the previous backup with the log archive gives the same result with almost the same effort.

Recovery from a node failure combines instant restart and instant restore into instant failover. In contrast to prior techniques that require multiple up-to-date copies of the database, instant failover builds a new up-to-date copy of the database as guided by actual transactions and in the background. This reduces the vulnerability during recovery, because both traditional mirroring and traditional log shipping are down by one copy after a failure whereas instant failover never is.

Instant recovery reduces not only downtime but also hardware requirements. A promising next step exploits instant failover to reduce the number of nodes required in a data center. Instead of one or multiple stand-by nodes for each active node, e.g., 3N nodes including N active nodes, a shared pool of just a few stand-by nodes may be equipped with access to database backups and log archives on shared storage. Note that, once failover has occurred, the active database and the active recovery log may be local to the new active node. The great advantage of the design is that it requires merely a few shared stand-by nodes, e.g., N+3 nodes including N active nodes. For a data center with N=100 or more active nodes, the change from 3N to N+3 permits substantial savings from infrastructure to power consumption.

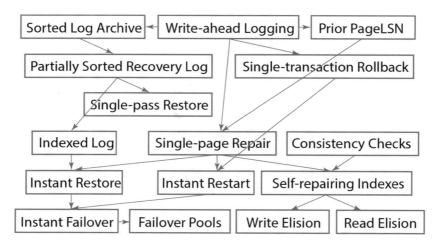

Figure 16.1: Recovery techniques and their dependencies.

Figure 16.1 illustrates relationships among many of the techniques introduced by this research. Traditional techniques such as write-ahead logging and exactly-once "redo" are crucial components of the family of techniques called instant recovery. The core enabling technology is single-page repair as a complement to single-transaction rollback—together, these two techniques permit incremental, on-demand recovery from system failures (software crashes), media failures (hardware faults), and node failures (including network disconnect). Another core technique is sorting the log archive—it enables not only single-pass restore but also instant backups and virtual backups and it renders incremental backups as well as frequent full backups obsolete. Finally, indexing backups and the log archive enables incremental, on-demand restore logic for instant restore, instant failover, and instant failback. The latter two of these in turn enable elastic database clusters with stateful nodes as well as failover pools with only a handful of stand-by failover destination and thus data centers shrunk to a fraction of their traditional sizes.

Table 16.1 summarizes the main differences in the recovery algorithms of traditional (ARIES) recovery and instant recovery. For single-page failures, the per-page chain of log records within the recovery log enables efficient single-page repair. For system failures, instant restart enables new transactions soon after reboot—fewer than a failure-free system but more than a system entirely occupied with "redo" and "undo" recovery. For media failures, a partially sorted log archive enables single-pass restore, i.e., re-creation of an up-to-date, transactionally correct database copy in a time similar to the first of five phases in traditional restore operations. Moreover, using indexes on backups and on runs in the partially sorted log archive, instant restore enables new transactions very soon after provisioning a formatted but empty replacement device. For node failures, instant failover enables new transactions very soon after failover to a node with access to an indexed backup and log archive but without the need for its own up-to-date database copy. Instant failover reduces pre-failure activities on secondary nodes, perceived mean time to repair after a node or communication failure, and vulnerability to data loss during recovery from a node or communication failure. Finally, this book also introduces multiple variants and applications for each of these techniques.

| Table 16.1: Individual techniques in ARIES recovery and in instant recovery | | | |
|---|---|---|---|
| | **Traditional (ARIES)** | **Instant Recovery** | **Purpose, Advantage, Comments** |
| **Logging** | | | |
| Chain of log records | Per transaction | Per database page | For single-page repair |
| Pointer in rollback log records | Next undo LSN | Original log record | Small rollback log record |
| Database representation changes | Top-level actions | System transactions | |
| **Restart after a system failure** | | | |
| Log scan for log analysis | Forward, checkpoint to end-of-log | Backward, end-of-log to checkpoint | Avoids pointer the last good checkpoint |
| Restart "redo" logic | By log scan | Page-by-page | Incremental and parallel "redo" and "undo" |
| Restart "undo" logic | By log scan | Transaction-by-transaction | |
| Lock re-acquisition | During "redo" | During log analysis | Earlier new transactions |
| New transactions | After "redo" | After log analysis | |
| First new checkpoint | | | Fast 2nd restart if required |
| **Restore after a media failure** | | | |
| Log archive organization | Original sequence of log records | Sorted into runs | Single-pass aggregation during log archiving |
| Restore phases | Full restore, differential restore, incremental restore, log analysis, log replay ("redo"), rollback ("undo") | | Single-pass merge during instant restore, run incrementally guided by active transactions |
| Backup creation | From active database | Merging old backup and log archive partitions | No load on database server |

| Failover after a node failure or a communication failure | | | |
|---|---|---|---|
| Network traffic prior to failover | Log records (in log shipping) or entire database pages (in mirroring) | Log records (log shipping) | |
| Activity on secondary nodes prior to failover | Maintain up-to-date database copy | Append log records to log archive, including run generation and indexing | No up-to-date database copy required |
| Activity after failover | Create new database copy, ship out new log records | Ship new log records | Copying requires bandwidth |
| Vulnerability to data loss during recovery | "Down by one copy" until new up-to-date database copy is complete | Instant recovery incrementally creates a new database copy from backup and log archive | Vulnerability to data loss during recovery equal to a failure-free system |

# References

[A 03] Lars Arge: The buffer tree: a technique for designing batched external data structures. *Algorithmica* 37(1): 1–24 (2003). DOI: 10.1007/s00453-003-1021-x. 31

[BD 83] Dina Bitton, David J. DeWitt: Duplicate record elimination in large data files. *ACM TODS* 8(2): 255–265 (1983). DOI: 10.1145/319983.319987. 57

[BG 88] Dina Bitton, Jim Gray: Disk shadowing. *VLDB* 1988: 331–338. 11

[CDF 94] Michael J. Carey, David J. DeWitt, Michael J. Franklin, Nancy E. Hall, Mark L. McAuliffe, Jeffrey F. Naughton, Daniel T. Schuh, Marvin H. Solomon, C. K. Tan, Odysseas G. Tsatalos, Seth J. White, Michael J. Zwilling: Shoring up persistent applications. *ACM SIGMOD* 1994: 383–394. DOI: 10.1145/191839.191915. 10

[CLG 94] Peter M. Chen, Edward K. Lee, Garth A. Gibson, Randy H. Katz, David A. Patterson: RAID: high-performance, reliable secondary storage. *ACM Comput. Surv.* 26(2): 145–185 (1994). DOI: 10.1145/176979.176981. 11

[G 78] Jim Gray: Notes on data base operating systems. Advanced course on operating systems. *Springer LNCS* #60, 1978: 393–481. 7, 13, 14, 50

[G 03] Goetz Graefe: Sorting and indexing with partitioned b-trees. *CIDR* 2003. 16

[G 04] Goetz Graefe: Write-optimized b-trees. *VLDB* 2004: 672–683. 21

[G 07] Goetz Graefe: Hierarchical locking in b-tree indexes. *BTW* 2007: 18–42. 44

[G 09] Goetz Graefe: The five-minute rule 20 years later (and how flash memory changes the rules). *CACM* 52(7): 48–59 (2009). DOI: 10.1145/1538788.1538805. 43

[G 12] Goetz Graefe: A survey of b-tree logging and recovery techniques. *ACM TODS* 37(1): 1 (2012). DOI: 10.1145/2109196.2109197. 18, 22

[GCG 14] Aakash Goel, Bhuwan Chopra, Ciprian Gerea, Dhrúv Mátáni, Josh Metzler, Fahim Ul Haq, Janet L. Wiener: Fast database restarts at Facebook. *ACM SIGMOD* 2014: 541–549. DOI: 10.1145/2588555.2595642. 1

[GK 12] Goetz Graefe, Harumi A. Kuno: Definition, detection, and recovery of single-page failures, a fourth class of database failures. *PVLDB* 5(7): 646–655 (2012). 2, 21, 28

[GK 15] Goetz Graefe, Hideaki Kimura: Orthogonal key-value locking. *BTW* 2015: 237–256. 44

[GKK 12] Goetz Graefe, Hideaki Kimura, Harumi A. Kuno: Foster b-trees. *ACM TODS* 37(3): 17 (2012). DOI: 10.1145/2338626.2338630. 22, 27, 60

[GKS 12] Goetz Graefe, Harumi A. Kuno, Bernhard Seeger: Self-diagnosing and self-healing indexes. *DBTest* 2012: 8. DOI: 10.1145/2304510.2304521. 27

[GLK 13] Goetz Graefe, Mark Lillibridge, Harumi A. Kuno, Joseph Tucek, Alistair C. Veitch: Controlled lock violation. *ACM SIGMOD* 2013: 85-96. DOI: 10.1145/2463676.2465325. 48

[GS 09] Goetz Graefe, Ryan Stonecipher: Efficient verification of b-tree integrity. *BTW* 2009: 27–46. 21, 22, 60

[GS 13] Goetz Graefe, Bernhard Seeger: Logical recovery from single-page failures. *BTW* 2013: 113–132. 23

[HR 83] Theo Härder, Andreas Reuter: Principles of transaction-oriented database recovery. *ACM Comput. Surv.* 15(4): 287–317 (1983). DOI: 10.1145/289.291. 5

[JPH 09] Ryan Johnson, Ippokratis Pandis, Nikos Hardavellas, Anastasia Ailamaki, Babak Falsafi: Shore-MT: a scalable storage manager for the multicore era. *EDBT* 2009: 24–35. DOI: 10.1145/1516360.1516365. 10

[L 93] David B. Lomet: Key range locking strategies for improved concurrency. *VLDB* 1993: 655–664. 44

[LG 98] Per-Åke Larson, Goetz Graefe: Memory management during run generation in external sorting. *ACM SIGMOD* 1998: 472–483. DOI: 10.1145/276305.276346. 52

[LY 81] Philip L. Lehman, S. Bing Yao: Efficient locking for concurrent operations on b-trees. *ACM TODS* 6(4): 650–670 (1981). DOI: 10.1145/319628.319663. 28, 60

[M 90] C. Mohan: ARIES/KVL: a key-value locking method for concurrency control of multiaction transactions operating on b-tree indexes. *VLDB* 1990: 392–405. 7, 44

[M 90b] C. Mohan: Commit_LSN: a novel and simple method for reducing locking and latching in transaction processing systems. *VLDB* 1990: 406–418. 8

[M 93] C. Mohan: A cost-effective method for providing improved data availability during DBMS restart recovery after a failure. *VLDB* 1993: 368–379. 8, 10, 43

[M 95] C. Mohan: Disk read-write optimizations and data integrity in transaction systems using write-ahead logging. *ICDE* 1995: 324–331. 21

[M 06] J. E. B. Moss: Open nested transactions: semantics and support. Workshop on memory performance issues (WMPI), Austin, TX, 2006. 8

[M 12] Microsoft "Restore (Transact-SQL)" http://technet.microsoft.com/en-us/library/ms186858.aspx, see also: http://technet.microsoft.com/en-us/library/ms175168.aspx. 14

[MHL 92] C. Mohan, Donald J. Haderle, Bruce G. Lindsay, Hamid Pirahesh, Peter M. Schwarz: ARIES: a transaction recovery method supporting fine-granularity locking and partial rollbacks using write-ahead logging. *ACM TODS* 17(1): 94–162 (1992). DOI: 10.1145/128765.128770. 7, 10, 47, 86

[ML 92] C. Mohan, Frank E. Levine: ARIES/IM: an efficient and high concurrency index management method using write-ahead logging. *ACM SIGMOD* 1992: 371–380. 7

[MN 93] C. Mohan, Inderpal Narang: An efficient and flexible method for archiving a database. *ACM SIGMOD* 1993: 139–146. 12

[MP 91] C. Mohan, Hamid Pirahesh: ARIES-RRH: restricted repeating of history in the ARIES transaction recovery method. *IEEE ICDE* 1991: 718–727. DOI: 10.1109/ICDE.1991.131521. 39, 53

[O 92] Patrick E. O'Neil: The SB-tree: an index-sequential structure for high-performance sequential access. *Acta Inf.* 29(3): 241–265 (1992). DOI: 10.1007/BF01185680. 23

[S 05] Lee Siegmund: DB2 for z/OS High availability and unplanned outage recovery. *IBM Systems Magazine*, November 2005. 14, 57

[SK 07] Jayson Speer, Markus Kirchberg: C-ARIES: A multi-threaded version of the ARIES recovery algorithm. *DEXA* 2007: 319–328. 8

# Author Biographies

**Goetz Graefe** has been a professor, product architect, and industrial researcher since 1987. Like other database vendors, Microsoft SQL Server adopted his designs for query optimization and query execution. He has published tutorial surveys on query execution, sorting, b-tree indexing, concurrency control, logging and recovery, as well as numerous novel techniques and research results in query processing and transactional data storage.

**Wey Guy** is an independent software engineer. She earned a Master's degree in computer science from the University of Iowa and spent 15 years with Microsoft's SQL Server development team before she became an independent software developer in 2011. She has been working with Hewlett Packard Labs since 2012.

**Caetano Sauer** is a doctoral candidate in computer science at the Technical University of Kaiserslautern, Germany. He earned his M.Sc. degree in 2012 at the same institution. While his interests and experience cover all components of transactional storage and indexing, his research focuses on logging and recovery algorithms. He is advised by Prof. Theo Härder and Dr. Goetz Graefe.

Printed in the United States
by Baker & Taylor Publisher Services